CONNECTIONS AND PARALLELS
BETWEEN HUMANISTIC PSYCHOLOGY
AND MODERN DANCE AT JACOB'S PILLOW

Connections and Parallels Between Humanistic Psychology and Modern Dance at Jacob's Pillow

Hadassah H. Hoffman

Studies in Dance
Volume 4

The Edwin Mellen Press
Lewiston•Queenston•Lampeter

Library of Congress Cataloging-in-Publication Data

Hoffman, Hadassah H.
    Connections and parallels between humanistic psychology and modern dance at Jacob's Pillow / Hadassah H. Hoffman.
        p. cm. -- (Studies in dance ; v. 4)
    Includes bibliographical references and index.
    ISBN 0-7734-6226-0
    1. Modern dance--Psychological aspects. 2. Humanistic psychology. I. Jacob's Pillow Dance Festival. II. Title. III. Series.

GV1588.5.H64 2004
792.8'01'9--dc22

                                                                    2004061791

This is volume 4 in the continuing series
Studies in Dance
Volume 4 ISBN 0-7734-6226-0
SD Series ISBN 0-7734-7742-X

A CIP catalog record for this book is available from the British Library

Front cover illustration: An original drawing by Arthur S. Hoffman

Copyright © 2004   Hadassah H. Hoffman

The Edwin Mellen Press   The Edwin Mellen Press
        Box 450   Box 67
Lewiston, New York   Queenston, Ontario
   USA 14092-0450   CANADA L0S 1L0

The Edwin Mellen Press, Ltd.
Lampeter, Ceredigion, Wales
UNITED KINGDOM SA48 8LT

Printed in the United States of America

My thanks to those ten pioneers of American modern dance, who have brought beauty and joy into our lives for the past 50 years. They graciously contributed their time to become participants in this study, and agreed to permit me to acknowledge them here: Mary Anthony, Robbie Barnett, Trisha Brown, Carmen deLavallade, Phyllis Lamhut, Murray Louis, Daniel Nagrin, Don Redlich, Jennifer Scanlon, and Glen Tetley.

And my appreciation to the entire Hoffman family, who endured my absence in body, mind, and spirit on countless occasions: To Arthur, Rachel, and Douglas, to Tina, Johanna, and Joda, and to Michael and Juliet Gabrielle.

CONTENTS

TABLES

.

FOREWORD

This study was undertaken because of the similarities between the evolution of humanistic psychology and the development of American modern dance. Humanistic psychology and modern dance both emphasized the need for personal liberation, and both represented a rebellious response to the status quo, one in the field of psychology, and the other in the American dance world.

Because of this parallel process, the research question has several aspects: first, did the growth of either humanistic psychology or modern dance assist the other to evolve? Second, what were the significant connections that were made between the pioneers in each of these fields? What awareness did the psychologists and dancers have of each other's work? Did the dance/movement therapists provide connections? Finally, were the evolutions of humanistic psychology and American modern dance reflective of the vast cultural shifts that were occurring throughout the western world during the first part of the 20th century?

The research methodology combines two approaches. An archival, database literature review examines the work of four pioneers of humanistic psychology, Abraham Maslow, Rollo May, Carl Rogers, and James Bugental. A similar literature review explores the writings of the dancers Ted Shawn, Ruth St. Denis, Mary Wigman, Martha Graham, and Hanya Holm, and the work of the dance/movement therapists, Marian Chace, Penny Bernstein Lewis, Fran Levy, and Ilene Serlin. Both reviews situate the exploration within a sociopolitical context.

The second research approach contains 10 semi-structured interviews, conducted with contemporary modern dancers about their professional work, their teachers, their knowledge of and experience with psychology and psychotherapy, and their connections to Jacob's Pillow Dance Festival. The 10 interviews were coded for themes and ideas, and presented in a case-ordered meta-matrix. The matrix display provided a data reduction tool, permitting data verification and the determination of conclusions.

The research results demonstrate an evolving interest, along generational lines, among the dancers, the four pioneers of humanistic psychology, and the dance/movement therapists. It was within the third generation that the strongest connections between the groups emerged.

It is also the third generation that is the most reflective of the changing zeitgeist during the 20th century. This study discusses the pioneers in these three fields, hoping to demonstrate the parallel growth and evolution that occurred.

PREFACE

The 20th century will be remembered for the variety and range of its discoveries, innovations and new ideas. The sciences produced electricity for the masses, radio, television, and finally the computer. Medicine developed life-saving vaccines, techniques to promote health and longevity, and new ways to reduce suffering and hasten healing. Scientists learned how to split the atom, initiating the atomic age of weaponry. Others sent men to the moon and space vehicles into orbit for months at a time. Within one century, humankind developed the new skills to improve the quality of life and to extend life, but also the ability to destroy human life on the planet.

Equally important developments occurred in psychology and the expressive arts. In 1909, Sigmund Freud, Sandor Ferenczi, Ernest Jones, Carl Jung and others traveled to a conference at Clark University and introduced psychoanalysis to America. Their innovative ideas about the human psyche, the workings of the unconscious, and the relevance of dreams were foundational for the new field of psychology and psychotherapy. Philosophers, psychoanalysts, and psychologists debated and developed this field throughout the remainder of the 20th century. Concurrently, behaviorists developed their theories and methods of changing people. But some psychologists saw both psychoanalysis and behaviorism as reductionistic, insufficiently addressing human creativity and potential. Thus was humanistic psychology born, with help from European existentialist and students of creativity and self-actualization. It became known as the "third force" in psychology, and began to examine creativity, love, the hierarch of needs, and self-actualization.

The creative arts--music, art, dance and theater--were also evolving throughout the 20th century. Art moved from the representational to Surrealism, to Cubism, and into realms of abstractionism. As the field of dance developed throughout this period the pioneers traveled and assimilated new ideas and techniques from Europe and the orient. At first, in the 1920s, the pioneers borrowed the ideas of others to create new works. By the 1930s, American dance had become more specifically focused upon the American scene. Dances reflected the actions of farmers and home builders at work; other choreographers dealt with the stresses of an industrialized society and loss of personal freedoms. Modern dance, developing from ballet and ethnic dance, represented a third force within the field of dance, which became increasingly reflective of the contemporary environment.

Hadassah H. Hoffman, studying the ways in which humanistic psychology and modern dance developed, has produced an impressive study of these two fields and their relationship. She has documented the history of humanistic psychology, and in an effort to establish connections between humanistic psychology and modern dance, has researched the literature of dance/movement therapy as well. Her presentation of the biographies of the pioneers of American modern dance, and her comprehensive history of Jacob's Pillow, is thorough and informative.

With much persistence and appreciative outreach, Dr. Hoffman secured interviews with a third generation of modern dancers, and these interviews add much liveliness to her study. The interviews are very personal and reflective of the ever-changing field of American modern dance. This fascinating work of cultural and personal history provides valuable and very human insights into how creative people and movements evolve. In a sense, the author has produced "a dance of ideas and the people who lived them."

Thomas Greening
Professor of Psychology
Saybrook Graduate School
Professor Greening is now in his 46th year of private practice of psychotherapy. He is not, however, a very good dancer.

ACKNOWLEDGMENTS

I would like to acknowledge the contribution of the many professionals who donated their time and energy to assist with this project. Special thanks goes to Norton Owen, Archivist and Director of Preservation at Jacob's Pillow, who provided the necessary background data, and access to the extensive Pillow archives. His knowledge and enthusiasm for this project have been an invaluable source of inspiration.

And to Tom Greening, Ph.D., Chairman, Stanley Krippner, Ph.D., and Ilene Serlin, Ph.D., A.D.T.R: I am grateful for your wisdom, patience, and your endless encouragement. You have contributed an immeasurable amount to the success of this project, and I could not have completed it without your support.

Chapter 1

Introduction

During my first year at Saybrook Graduate School, I was intrigued by an article in the *Journal of Humanistic Psychology,* "Deconstructing The Lone Genius Myth: Toward a Contextual View of Creativity" (Montuori & Purser, 1995). The thesis of this article was that "Creative expression always occurs within a cultural and historical milieu. Any discussion of creativity inevitably needs to be situated within a historical, but also a sociopolitical context" (1995, p. 71).

Since I was taking a course with Dr. Montuori at that time, we had several discussions about this article. I asked him whether he thought his ideas might have any relevance to the field of dance, specifically to the work of choreographers. Montuori was interested in this concept, especially when I discussed the work of George Balanchine. Balanchine was an outstanding 20th century ballet choreographer whose work might be understood as situated within a cultural context. Balanchine produced at least three distinct stylistic periods of work, which corresponded to his emigration from Russia and his subsequent travel: i.e., there was a Russian period between 1920-1924; a European period (primarily spent in France), which lasted until 1933; and the American period which stretched from 1934 until his death in 1983 (Taper, 1996). There had also been a Public Broadcasting System interview with Balanchine in which he discussed the ways in which music reflects the culture of the composer. Balanchine stated that he had employed music that illustrated these differences, citing his use of John Philip Sousa's marches for the ballet "Stars and Stripes Forever" because this music reflects the ways in which Americans walk and move.

Montuori challenged me to pursue these ideas, conceptualize them, and write about them. However, I was unclear at that time about how to explore these ideas, and where they might fit into my studies at Saybrook.

Subsequently, I spent two semesters studying how the neo-Freudians had influenced the development of humanistic psychology, by tracing the transmission of ideas from the neo-Freudians to Rollo May, Abraham Maslow, Carl Rogers, and James Bugental. Within that same period of time, I visited the Jacob's Pillow Dance Festival in Lee, Massachusetts, during its 65th anniversary season. While reading *A Certain Place: The Jacob's Pillow Story* (Owen, 1997), I was struck by the similarities between the development of modern dance and the evolution of humanistic psychology. Could parallels be drawn between the two evolutionary processes? Both modern dance and humanistic psychology share the same theoretical stance, i.e., the need for individual liberation.

For example, who were the originators of modern dance? I conceptualized that ballet and ethnic dance played a role in the development of modern dance, similar to the role psychoanalysis and behaviorism played in the growth of humanistic psychology. If the neo-Freudians were responsible for Americanizing psychoanalysis, who were the people in the field of modern dance who were responsible for Americanizing dance? And then, who were the people who transmitted the ideas from the initiators in modern dance, to the next generation of dancers?

Humanistic psychology evolved because a group of psychologists drew upon a long tradition linking psychology with the humanities and, in a rebellious manner, institutionally founded humanistic psychology. They regarded themselves as a "third force," alluding to the fact that they were an alternative to the dominant behavioristic and psychoanalytic orientation in psychology. (deCarvalho, 1991, p.1)

Modern dance and the modern dancers displayed a similar responsive impulse, a defiance of the status quo. The early modern dancers stressed personal freedom and a willingness to defy the conventions of their time.

Rebelliousness in American Dance

American modern dance is also a reflection of rebellion and represented an entirely new way of conceptualizing dance. One of the earliest examples of the rebelliousness of modern dance was the career of Isadora Duncan. Born in 1878, she died in a tragic accident in 1927 (McDonagh, 1976, p.15). She has been called the "mother" of American modern dance:

> In her endeavors to return through her dancing to the purity and harmony of Ancient Greece....She impressed herself on society as a serious artist, albeit a dancer. Duncan led an unconventional life, but she also thoroughly denied the aesthetic norms of her day....She challenged the very image of the dancer by refusing to adopt the ballet dancers 'look' for herself....By her very stance, the solidity of her presence, she affirmed her connection to the ground....Duncan was rounded where the ballet dancer was straight....She was monumental. (Siegel, 1979, pp.8-9)

Isadora Duncan made another important contribution to the history of modern dance through her commitment to teaching, and she established many schools throughout the world. She conceptualized her training for young people as more than merely teaching techniques.

> Isadora was interested in teaching philosophy, aesthetics and health. She wished to belong to history not only by means of theaters....or

reproductions of her performances, but through a legacy of action that other generations could carry on after her. (Siegel, 1979, p.10)

Ruth St. Denis was a contemporary of Isadora Duncan, who wrote about her and her work.

Duncan was, to those who had been fortunate to see her, a vivid echo of Greek loveliness. Her unforgettable power of stirring the mind to the idea of Greek culture, and her insistence upon the use of great music was reverberating in the artistic atmosphere of the dance....Duncan's return to the natural dance penetrated in less than one generation many phases of our development and gave us new standards of bodily normality. (St. Denis, 1939, p.92)

Isadora Duncan established certain themes in her work, which would be carried on by other pioneers in the field. She was inspired by the Greek myths and brought them into her dances. The Duncan "look" was that of a fully developed, strong woman, feet firmly planted upon the earth. Finally, she developed a series of schools for her students and for the next generations. She sought to teach not only dance techniques, but her own version of philosophy, health, and aesthetics. She was the first of the great rebels in the field of American modern dance.

Ruth St. Denis was a contemporary of Isadora Duncan, who was born in 1879 and died in 1968. Her collaboration with her husband, Ted Shawn, produced the Denishawn Company. The Denishawn Company, under the leadership of St. Denis and Shawn, opened its school in Los Angeles in 1915. It presented an artistic creed, which was to guide the Denishawn school and the company (which toured throughout the world for the next 16 years).

The area of the dance is too big to be encompassed by any one system. The dance includes all systems or schools of dance. Every way that any human being of any race or nationality...has moved rhythmically to express himself, belongs to the dance. We endeavor to recognize and use all contributions of the past to the dance and will continue to include all new contributions in the future. (Terry, 1976, p.67)

Ted Shawn continued to be an innovator and after the Denishawn era ended he purchased Jacob's Pillow. He had another vision of what American dance could become

One of the most fascinating chapters in modern dance history began at Jacob's Pillow in 1933 when the Men Dancers came into being. Shawn invited six young men to launch this new venture which was intended to make the case for dancing as a legitimate career for American men. (Owen, 1997, p.9)

In the early decades of the 20th century, there was only one male dance star, and that was Ted Shawn. He stood alone and won acceptance for himself. When he originated the Men Dancers at Jacob's Pillow he was initiating a new role, a new function for men who danced. Traditionally, men had served as partners to women dancers, with the occasional opportunity to star in a *pas de deux* within a classical ballet.

Shawn's desire to shift the role of men dancers represented an important break with the traditions of dance. Another radical shift in the form of the dance evolved because of the primitive state of the original Jacob's Pillow site. The men who joined Shawn as dancers had to build their own cabins and raise their own food. Shawn, observing the men at work, incorporated the actions of construction, farming, and basic tasks of everyday life into his earliest choreography for the men dancers. He therefore broke new ground in dance in several ways, expanding the parameters of what had been dance.

As modern dance was evolving during the 1930s, humanistic psychology was also developing. This development was partially due to the advent of the neo-Freudians, who helped to Americanize psychoanalysis. It is possible to review these two distinct evolutionary processes that occurred at approximately the same time. It is also possible to trace the beginnings of humanistic psychology back into the early part of the 20th century by reading the work of Sandor Ferenczi. Ferenczi was a colleague of Sigmund Freud, whose innovative ideas led him far from the traditional psychoanalytic orthodoxy. This research attempts to discover whether there are any connections and parallels between the development of humanistic psychology and the evolution of modern dance in America.

Rationale and Objectives

The main objectives of this study are to explore whether, and in what ways, the process of growth in one field paralleled and enhanced the development of the other. Did the growth of humanistic psychology have an impact upon modern dance as it evolved through Jacob's Pillow? Did the psychologists have an impact upon the dancers? Did the dancers contribute their knowledge and perceptions to the psychologists? What part did the dance therapists play, if any?

The second objective is to gather sufficient information (by means of extensive archival and database literature reviews and a series of in-depth research interviews) about the development of humanistic psychology and the evolution of modern dance. The purpose of this is to develop an understanding of the importance of both of these phenomena as instances of rebellion and dissent.

A third objective is to identify and explore any mutual influences that might have occurred between the participants within these evolutionary processes. Although the psychologists did not generally discuss dance or dancing, did they have any knowledge of modern dance, or the dancers themselves? And what did the dancers know about psychology, and this group of psychologists? Did the dance therapists contribute to this exchange of knowledge?

The purpose of this study is to make a small contribution to the evolving literature currently being written about the culture of the 20th century. I examined the evolutionary processes in the fields of psychology and modern dance, in an exploration that bears some similarity to the work of Helen Thomas (1995), author of *Dance Modernity and Culture*, and to Jack Anderson's *Art Without Boundaries* (1997).

Chapter 2

Review of the Literature

Archival and database research methods comprise one significant aspect of the methodology employed in this study. The research interviews represent the other methodology. The procedures that were utilized are discussed at length in the methodology section of this study.

In 1999, I completed a pilot study for my research practicum which included an interview of Anna Halprin. Halprin is a famous West Coast dancer, and the focus of this study was to explore the connections between her and Fritz Perls. The central questions were, did Halprin make any contributions to Perls' innovative work in Gestalt psychology, and did Perls' ideas contribute to her work as a dancer?

Halprin was interviewed by telephone in a semi-structured interview format. The transcription of the interview was then coded for themes, and the findings were presented in the practicum summary. I learned many significant lessons about research interviewing during this process. The actual interview was too long for the participant, and she terminated the conversation before I had addressed the central questions. Also, the researcher did not follow up on several important leads that developed during the interview, which closed off access to potential information. I also had done an inadequate literature review, and had missed out on materials that Halprin had written, and that others had written about her work.

This interview led to the discovery of several important pieces of information. Halprin believed that she had contributed to the work of Perls, because she had shown him how to integrate movement into his work. She also acknowledged that she had learned a great deal of psychology from him, which added new dimensions to her own work. Another relevant piece of information was uncovered during the course of the interview. Although Halprin had lived on the East Coast, had performed in New York City, and had studied with many modern dance pioneers at the American Dance Festival, she had no connections to Jacob's Pillow. For this reason, she was not included as a participant in this research inquiry (Hoffman, 1999a).

This study first reviews the work of four pioneers of humanistic psychology: Abraham Maslow, Rollo May, Carl Rogers, and James Bugental. An extensive review of the literature was previously conducted, which explored some of the historical precedents leading to the development of humanistic psychology. This review was discussed in the article, "Sandor Ferenczi and the Origins of Humanistic Psychology," (Hoffman, 2003). It included the work of the neo-Freudian generation of psychotherapists, including Andras Angyal, Izette deForest, Erich Fromm, Frieda Fromm-Reichmann, Karen Horney, Harry Stack Sullivan, and Clara Thompson. This background material is referenced throughout this study.

The second portion of the literature review includes the autobiographies and biographies of Ted Shawn, Ruth St. Denis, Martha Graham, Mary Wigman, and Hanya Holm. The archives at Jacob's Pillow provided an extensive dissertation on Ted Shawn, which is discussed here.

The final segment of the literature review explores the writings of dance therapists, such as Marian Chace, Penny Bernstein Lewis, Fran Levy, and Ilene Serlin. The essay "Marian Chace: The Bridge Between Dance and Psychology" (Hoffman, 1999c), contains an extensive exploration of the dance therapy literature.

There is historical precedent for connecting an art form and the field of psychology. In fact, two Saybrook graduates utilized their dissertations to make such unusual explorations into this new territory. In 1976, Frederick Gilbert wrote a dissertation at Saybrook Graduate School (then Humanistic Psychology Institute) on *Jazz, Rock and Roll, and the Revolution in Psychotherapy*. Gilbert's thesis was that

> Popular music and psychotherapy are both cultural forms that are responsive to, and reflect larger social evolution....In particular, it is possible to see through the data presented here how changes in musical forms often precede changes that will occur in other social institutions or processes. (Gilbert, 1976, pp.17-18)

Another early Saybrook student, Penny Bernstein Lewis, agreed that "Dance therapy emerged gradually with a firm grounding in the world of dance and psychology" (Bernstein, 1979, p.5). Her book, *Eight Theoretical Approaches in Dance-Movement Therapy* (1979), was based upon her dissertation, entitled *Towards an Implicit Theory of Dance-Movement Therapy*, and was written under the chairmanship of Rollo May.

This pioneering work by Saybrook students in the 1970s was followed by other authors, who wrote about modern dance and its place within contemporary culture. In 1979, two important studies were published; the first edition of *The Vision of Modern Dance: In the Words of its Creators*, (Brown, Mindlin & Woodford), and *The Shapes of Change: Images of American Dance* (Siegel).

In 1987, *Dance and the Lived Body* by Sondra H. Fraleigh clearly linked the development of modern dance to existentialism. She stated, "Modern dance entered the American theater as boldly and as 'ungracefully' (some critics thought) as modern existentialism entered the American consciousness, and at roughly the same time" (Fraleigh, 1987, p. xxxii)

In her introduction, Fraleigh linked two specific concepts to her theory of dance aesthetics, notably embodiment, and the human drive towards creativity and mental health (Fraleigh, 1987, p. xvii). Abraham Maslow was the humanistic psychologist who studied the impact of creativity upon personal well-being. James Bugental focused upon the importance of embodiment to mental health in his book, *The Search for Authenticity: An Existential Approach to Psychotherapy* (1981). These two themes are discussed at greater length in the section on the humanistic psychologists.

The literature review reveals that the connections between modern dance and psychology were being discussed by several authors. These authors also placed modern dance within the context of contemporary culture. This research study expands upon these concepts and examines these ideas further.

Humanistic Psychology

Abraham Maslow. Abraham Maslow is the first of the four pioneers of humanistic psychology whose writings are reviewed here. An extended search of the PSYCINFO database, plus additional extensive bibliographies that appeared in *The Founders of Humanistic Psychology* (deCarvalho, 1991), *The Right To Be Human* (Hoffman, 1988), and other compilations of writings form this database about humanistic psychology.

Abraham Maslow was born in 1908 and died in 1970. "In the mid-1950s, Maslow began to acquire a national reputation outside the academic world for his work on creativity" (Hoffman, 1988, p.236). In 1959, Maslow delivered a lecture on creativity at Michigan State University, which was later published as "Creativity in Self-Actualizing People," in *Toward a Psychology of Being* (Maslow, 1986, pp.135-145). In this article, Maslow explored many of his ideas about creativity: "I first had to change my ideas about creativity as soon as I began studying people who were positively healthy, highly evolved and matured, self-actualizing" (p.135).

Maslow continued to review what he had discovered about important aspects of the creative process by examining a variety of creative endeavors. Through this process, he discovered a humanistic, rather than a Freudian, perspective on creativity. "In any case, so far as SA [Self-actualizing] creativeness is concerned, it seems to come more immediately from a fusion of primary and secondary processes rather than from working through repressive control of forbidden impulses and wishes" (p.144).

Maslow (1961) continued to study creativity, building upon his ideas about creativity and health. His article on "Health as Transcendence of Environment," appeared in the first issue of *The Journal of Humanistic Psychology.*

> Because the roots of ill health were found in the unconscious it has been our tendency to think of the unconscious as bad, evil, crazy...and to think of the primary processes as *distorting* the truth. But now that we have found these depths to be also the source of creativeness, of art, of love, of humor and play, we can begin to speak of a healthy unconscious, of healthy regression....Expressive behavior is either unmotivated or, less motivated than coping behavior....Expressive behaviors have little to do with environment and do not have the purpose of changing it or adapting to it.

> But more important is my preliminary finding that this kind of cognition of Being...of the world is found more often in healthy people and may even turn out to be one of the defining characteristics of health. (pp.4-6)

Maslow became increasingly involved in the study of creativity during the last decade of his life. "The Creative Attitude" was first published in a Canadian journal and was reprinted posthumously in *The Farther Reaches of Human Nature* (1971). In this article, Maslow reflected upon the connections between creativity and psychological well-being, and advocated a holistic approach to exploring creativity. He presented new ways of conceptualizing creativity. "I raise the question again of creativeness being an aspect of practically any behavior at all, whether perceptual or attitudinal or emotional, conative, cognitive or expressive" (p.77). The expansiveness of Maslow's work on creativity reflects an important attribute of humanistic thinking, which emphasizes many aspects of mental health and wellness, rather than the psychoanalytic focus upon curing " mental illnesses."

It was in this article that I located Maslow's only reference to dance or dancing. He proposed that there were different ways in which one might learn how to be a good dancer:

> Most people in an ad hoc society would go to the Arthur Murray School where you first move your left foot and then your right foot three paces and bit by bit you go through a lot of external, willed motions....We know that it is rather characteristic of successful psychotherapy that there are thousands of effects among which might well be good dancing, i.e., being more free about dancing, more graceful...less inhibited, less self conscious....In the same way, I think that psychotherapy, where it is good, and is successful, then psychotherapy...can be counted on to enhance the creativity of a person. (Maslow, 1971, p.78)

It was in this article that Maslow identified the improvisational characteristic that good dancers and good psychotherapists might share in common, and he understood several aspects of their creativity. The significance of this quote is that in it Maslow himself made the connection between dance and psychotherapy.

Maslow (1971) continued to expand his ideas on this subject, stating: These are some of the reasons why I consider nonverbal education so important, e.g., through art, through music, through dancing....What I am interested in is the new kind of education which we must develop which moves towards fostering the new kind of human being that we need, the process person, the creative person, the improvising person, the self trusting, courageous, the autonomous person. (p.100)

In this remarkable article, we observe Abraham Maslow improvising intellectually as he attempted to connect various aspects of creativity. It is striking that he continued to equate the psychologically healthy person with the creative person—a theme that continued to appear in his other posthumously published writing.

Maslow was profoundly interested in many aspects of creativity. He wrote extensively and delivered many lectures on this subject. He showed real comprehension of the importance of the experiential learning process, when he said: "Education through art is a kind of therapy and growth technique, because it permits the deeper layers of the psyche to emerge, and therefore to be encouraged, fostered, trained and educated" (1971, p.101).

My review of Maslow's work reveals that, with the one exception cited here, he made no other explicit connections between the worlds of psychology and dance. However, his extensive research on creativity led him to acknowledge the impact of experiential learning. He would probably have been a strong supporter of the creative arts therapies, that fusion between psychology and the arts.

Rollo May. Rollo May is the second of the four pioneers of humanistic psychology whose work is reviewed in this dissertation. Born in 1909, he died in 1994. In his obituary in *The New York Times*, May was acknowledged for being:

> ...one of the first thinkers in the field of psychotherapy to formulate a view of human nature that was not based upon Freudian principles....Dr. May was also one of the originators of the humanistic psychology movement, which concerns itself with the ways in which people can grow, and it avoids the Freudian approach of trying to heal personal difficulties that are residues of childhood. The movement blossomed in the 1960's and provided the intellectual platform for the human potential movement,

which also bloomed in that decade. (Pace, 1994, p.B12)

Rollo May was the author of more than a dozen books, a founding member of the Association of Humanistic Psychology, and the founder of American existential psychology. In 1987, May received the Gold Medal Award for Life Achievement from the American Psychological Association (Schneider & May, 1995, p.I).

On March 1, 2000, I wrote to his widow, Georgia May, and introduced myself, my proposed research topic and I requested a dialogue with her, either by telephone or in writing. Mrs. May called me on May 27th, leaving the message that "There was nothing in Dr. May's writing about dancing" (personal communication, May 27, 2000).

On February 28, 2000, I had a telephone conversation with Dr. Penny Bernstein Lewis, a Saybrook graduate, whose dissertation, *Toward an Implicit Theory of Dance-Movement Therapy* (1979), was written under the chairmanship of Rollo May. This dissertation was printed as *Eight Theoretical Approaches in Dance-Movement Therapy* (1979), and represented the first systematic attempt to discuss the differing theories employed by dance therapists. In our telephone conversation, Lewis began with this statement:

> I'm sorry I can't give you the information you were hoping for. Rollo May and I never spoke about dance or dance therapy, although he was my dissertation committee chair. We spoke about my ideas and my language, because he was trying to make me more clear and succinct. He was very supportive of my work.
>
> I would say that Rollo May was very connected with nature. I spent times with him at his home in Tiburon and also in New Hampshire. He seemed to be connected to the experience of physicality in nature. He was also very spiritual, and often quoted Paul Tillich, and referred to the spiritual exploration people go through during the latter part of their lives.

But he, himself, was not fully embodied. I mean that the body was not something that he necessarily responded to. For example, I was hugely pregnant during the time we were working on my dissertation, and he never once acknowledged it. Except that once, during my ninth month, he helped me out of a chair, but he never once said anything about my pregnancy. (personal communication, February 28, 2000)

When I questioned Lewis about Rollo May's silence as being reflective of his generation's reluctance to discuss a young woman's pregnancy or physical appearance, she agreed that this was certainly possible. She concluded with the observation, "I think that he selected me to work with because he knew me and my work, and it expanded his interest" (personal communication, February 28, 2000).

As a result of these two conversations, I began the literature review of May's books and articles with minimal expectations and scant hope of finding any material dealing with dance, or dancers. However, I was surprised to discover how much May had written about the body and indeed about dance.

Rollo May wrote extensively about creativity, and his 1975 book, *The Courage to Create* remains a classic on this subject. Although this book did not discuss dance per se, May's awareness of the body was made quite explicit, and in many different contexts. In the chapter, "Passion for Form," (May, 1975) wrote:

The importance of the forms is revealed in the inescapable unity of the body with the world....Whenever I walk, my body is interrelated with the world in which and on which I take my steps. This presupposes some harmony between body and world....The balance essential in walking is one that is not solely in my body; it can be understood only as a relationship of my body to the ground on which it stands and walks. The earth is there to meet each foot as it falls, and the rhythm of my walking depends upon my faith that the earth will be there. (p. 130)

When May reflected upon the nature of creativity, he postulated that the creative act itself was

An encounter between two poles....World is interrelated with the person at every moment....The pole of the world is an inseparable part of the creativity of an individual. What occurs is always a process, a doing–specifically a process interrelating the person and his or her world. (p.50)

Furthermore, May had strong convictions about the importance of art and its connections to the society in which it was created. He thought that art expressed the essence of any given period of time, because of the nature of the creative process, and he stated:

If you wish to understand the psychological and spiritual temper of any given historical period, you can do no better than to look long and searchingly at its art. For in the art the underlying spiritual meaning of the period is expressed directly in its symbols....They have the power to reveal the underlying meaning of any given period precisely because the essence of art is the powerful and alive encounter between the artist and his or her world. (p.52)

May extended these theories further, so as to place the artist firmly within an historical and cultural context. He stated firmly, "Genuine artists are so bound up with their age, that they cannot communicate separated from it. In this sense, too, the historical situation conditions the creativity" (p.54).

May continued his reflections about the connections between the arts and the society in which these arts were created in a later book, *My Quest for Beauty,* which was published in 1985. He lamented the state of contemporary life when he stated:

Art—in which we include along with painting and sculpture, the dance, architecture, literature, poetry, music—is devoted to the quality of human life. Hence the great confusion in art in our time: it is as though art is lost, it has no central soul or direction in which to go. (May, 1985, p.199)

Furthermore, in *My Quest for Beauty*, May wrote quite explicitly about the connections he had made between art and the human body. He stated that "Beauty reveals a form in the universe—the harmony of the spheres....It is a form which is felt in the curves and balance and our own bodies" (p.137).

When May viewed Mount Blanc, he was struck by its changing sense of body. He wrote that "The mountain form seemed to be painted on a canvas, it was disembodied, pure form with no weight or movement....The vast mountain took on a body, now organic, three-dimensional. It became a new being on a new level" (p.206).

In this statement, May utilized the concept of the body to symbolize the form he found in objects of great beauty. The body could represent a three-dimensional object, which might lend new shape and form.

May valued dance for another reason as well. He wrote about an experience that he'd had when in Switzerland, and was trying to sketch the designs on the stockings and skirts of a group of folk dancers. He was initially an observer of the scene, and to his surprise, became a participant when he became one of the dancers:

I shall never forget the experience of being whirled around by a peasant girl who did not come up to my shoulder but was, through long working in the fields and milking cows, as strong as the proverbial ox. It seems one can pick up the art of a village through one's bodily participation in its ceremonies. (p.15)

Although May did not expand upon this experience theoretically, his articulation and appreciation of what could be transmitted nonverbally is significant. He had learned the about the depth and breadth that is the potential of a group movement experience. And as May (1975) had written previously, "Out of the encounter is born the work of art" (p.85). One might wonder whether May would have felt that his encounter, within the context of a folk dance, could be considered a work of art.

In 1969, May published *Love and Will*, a book in which he discussed many of his ideas about sex, Eros, and the body. He lamented the objectification of sexuality by the researcher, Kinsey, and the clinicians, Masters and Johnson, stating, "We are in flight from Eros—and we use sex as a vehicle for the flight" (p.65). He reminded us that "Sex can be defined fairly adequately in physiological terms as consisting of the building up of bodily tensions and their release" (p.73).

May's discussions in *Love and Will* were frequently focused upon the need for reconnection between the body and the mind. He reflected his dismay at the lack of the emotional component in many contemporary sexual encounters. He offered a definition of the new Puritanism: "First, a state of alienation from the body. Second, the separation of emotion from reason. And third, the use of the body as a machine" (p.45).

May (1969) continued to explore the dangers of this lack of connection, both for the individual, and ultimately, for the relationship involved. He lamented

But there comes a point...when the cult of [sexual] technique destroys feeling, undermines passion, and blots out individual identity. The technologically efficient lover, defeated in the contradiction which is copulation without Eros, is ultimately the impotent one. He has lost the power to be carried away; he knows only too well what he is doing. At this point, technology diminishes consciousness and demolishes Eros. (p.97)

In this passage, Rollo May regretted the loss of the bodily feelings that might lead to ecstasy in favor of an expertise and facility in sexual techniques.

May's greatest concern was that the alienation from the body would permit only mechanistic functioning, and would create a permanent separation from Eros and true sexual fulfillment. As a psychotherapist and trainer of therapists, May knew that the connections between the body, the mind, and the emotions were essential, and that this connection also extends to the therapeutic process.

In an earlier article, May (1966) explored the links between the physical body and intentionality:

> What about the relation of the body to intentionality? When a patient…is blocked off from his wishes and intentionality in general, a good place to start is for the therapist simply to help the patient become aware of his bodily feeling at that moment.

> The body is the language of intentionality. Subtle gestures of the patient, his way of walking, whether he leans toward us or away at a particular moment in this session, all comprise a language of which he is unaware. But it may indeed tell us more accurately what's going on than what he articulates. (p.65)

Once again, Rollo May highlighted the nonverbal messages that could be received by the observant person (in this case, the therapist). He expanded the parameters of these observations by referring to the ideas of Harry Stack Sullivan and Frieda Fromm-Reichmann, both of whom had written about the role of empathy in the therapeutic situation. May (1966) wrote,

> I believe it can be said…that empathy operates on the level of intentionality…. the totality of what the other person thinks-feels-and-acts ('act' in the sense of how his body is oriented) is what we pick up….Empathy…is chiefly a feeling experience. (p.68).

May reminded us further that, as Fromm-Reichmann said,

> She could often tell by her own feelings what was going on in the patient, which the patient is unable…to express or even to recognize. The therapist often finds that his own feelings are his best instrument in doing therapy; and this is because by way of feeling or empathy, he can pick up the intentionality of his patient. (p.69)

The point that May continued to make in his books and articles was that the body presents messages of intentionality non verbally for the therapist to observe and to interpret. These ideas were historically very important: the concept of empathic listening originated in the writings of Sandor Ferenczi, and were transmitted into the next generation by the neo-Freudians, Harry Stack Sullivan, and Frieda Fromm-Reichmann (Hoffman, 1999b). In one of his earliest books, *The Art of Counseling*, May (1939) devoted a chapter to "Empathy—Key to the Counseling Process." However, in this book, May gives credit for his ideas on empathy to Carl Jung and Otto Rank. Rank was a professional colleague of Ferenzci, collaborating with him on *The Development of Psychoanalysis* (Ferenczi & Rank, 1925). Jung was one of the earliest psychoanalytic thinkers, travelling to Clark University in 1909 with Sigmund Freud, Sandor Ferenczi, and Ernest Jones (Hale, 1995).

It was Marian Chace, the Denishawn dancer, who became the "mother" of Dance Therapy, who integrated the idea of empathy into movement terms. She wrote about her work in nonanalytic terms, but presented herself as *"being with the patients in movement"* [emphasis added]. Marian Chace was a student of Frieda Fromm-Reichmann and Harry Stack Sullivan at the Washington School of Psychiatry. She worked as a dance therapist for 20 years at Chestnut Lodge, which was directed by Frieda Fromm-Reichmann (Hoffman, 1999c).

Rollo May's conclusions about the importance of the body in the therapeutic situation reflected his knowledge and experience of the body-mind connection, a connection which had been overlooked by traditional psychoanalysis.

> I believe that the body must come back into psychoanalysis....The body must come back as the deeper expression of the symbolic meanings in the individual's life, the language of intentionality, expressed with the power that is given in bodily function. (May, 1966, p.66)

In this statement, May ignored the writings of Wilhelm Reich, whose *Character Analysis* (1945/1990) was strongly focused upon the body. Reich stressed that "the organismic orgone energy is the *physical reality which* corresponds to the classical, merely psychological concept of 'psychic energy,'" (Reich, 1945/1990, p.xii). However, Reich's writings were always presented from a psychoanalytic viewpoint, and May's work embodied a more humanistic stance.

Rollo May was deeply interested in many aspects of creativity, as was Abraham Maslow. However, May extended his interest into an exploration of the body, and into the physical aspects of creativity. He utilized the body as a metaphor in many of his writings, and stressed the physicality of human experience. He also wrote about dance as a way of understanding culture. Contrary to the statements from the personal communications received, Rollo May did write about dance and the importance of the body in psychotherapy, in love, and in the larger world of culture and art.

Carl Rogers. Carl Rogers was born in 1902 and died in 1987 at the age of 85. Rogers is the third of the founders of humanistic psychology to be explored in this literature review. Rogers was one of psychology's most prolific authors, writing 16 books and more than 200 professional articles. His books have been translated into 60 foreign languages (Kirschenbaum & Henderson, 1989, pp.xi-xii). The extent of his published work presented this researcher with great challenges.

In order to accomplish a thorough review of Rogers' material, I began with the chronological bibliography in deCaravalho's (1991) *The Foundations of Humanistic Psychology*, which included a list of Rogers' books, articles, and chapters from books. PsycINFO provided an additional list of articles in journals and book chapters dating from 1947.

Working with these two bibliographies, I was able to explore a great deal of Carl Rogers' written work in my search for references to the body, dance, or the use of movement within the therapeutic milieu. Because creativity has always been stressed as one aspect of humanistic psychology, Rogers' written work was also searched for these references.

What became clear is that although Carl Rogers frequently wrote about "movement," he was not referring to actual physical, bodily movement. Rogers wrote, "From feelings which are unrecognized, unowned, unexpressed, the client moves toward a flow in which ever-changing feelings are experienced in the moment, knowingly and acceptingly, and may be accurately expressed" (1958, p.144).

Dance therapists often discuss the conception of flow. In these instances, flow is defined as "how the body concentrates its exertion" (Dell, 1970, p.11) as it is preparing for, or is engaged in physical action. Rogers might have agreed with the concept of making his idea of flow into an embodied construct, but his writings do not reveal this. It is noteworthy that several of the dance/movement therapists (to be reviewed) employed the ideas of Rogers in their theoretical conceptualizations.

Rogers wrote with clarity, often with simplicity, and his ideas frequently sound as if they could be employed as the basis for a dance/movement therapy session. Rogers (1963) wrote a chapter for the book *Conflict and Creativity*, which provides an example of this type of writing. Rogers discussed what might occur when a therapist continues to reflect "consistent and unconditional positive regard for [a client] him and his feelings" (p.74). According to Rogers, the client would then move towards an acceptance of his/her self, with new self-respect and self care. This would necessitate increased personal responsibility for the self, and would allow the client to "move forward in the process of being free" (p.73).

One might envision a dance/movement therapy session in which the therapist mirrors the movements of the client, indicating complete acceptance and regard. From this acceptance, the client may move (literally) into new areas, both psychologically and physically, or might elect to repeat whatever feels liberating and personally valid. After all, Rogers (1986) specified, "In person-centered therapy, the person is free to choose any direction" (p.197). This exchange between client and therapist could be equally effective in either verbal or nonverbal therapeutic sessions. The goal for either therapist is similar: the client "…moves toward being more real….As these changes occur, as he becomes more self-aware, more self-acceptant, more self-expressive…he finds that he is at last free to change and grow in the directions natural to the human organism" (Rogers, 1963, p.75).

A dance/movement therapy session also focuses upon the client finding his or her own range of movement, developing a means of self-expression, and finding a personal direction or path. The similarities are clear and illustrate why so many dance/movement therapists have utilized Rogerian theories.

Rogers often discussed the movement of a client through the therapeutic process. One might question what his ideas and feelings were about actual physical movement within the therapeutic environment. He discussed his views about physical movement and contact within the group context. He stated that he always attempted to

Express myself in physical movements as spontaneously as possible. My background is not such as to make me particularly free in this respect. But if I am restless I get up and stretch and move around; if I want to change places with another person, I ask him if he is willing. One may sit or lie on the floor if that meets one's physical needs. I do not particularly attempt, however, to promote physical movement in others, though there are facilitators who can do this beautifully and effectively. (Rogers, 1970, p.58)

This statement illustrates Rogers' personal ambivalence about the use of physical movement during his group sessions. He tried to be spontaneous when he moved, but acknowledged a lack of comfort in doing do. He allowed himself to stretch and move about the room, or he would change places physically with another group member. What is lacking is permission for the other group members to move freely about the room, to change places because they elect to do so, or to initiate some type of movement in the group. His statement about sitting or lying on the floor is intriguing, because it is unclear whether it refers to a group member or to Rogers himself. One might contrast Rogers' ideas on this subject with the early writings of Sandor Ferenczi, who allowed his clients (patients) to pace freely about the room whenever they felt the need to do so (Ferenczi, 1929/1955, p.114).

Rogers was most comfortable speaking of movement through the therapeutic process as a nonphysical event. He did not criticize other facilitators who encourage and promote bodily movement during group sessions, which indicates his open admiration of those who could accomplish this. This reflects Rogers' remarkable openness to new ideas, and variations within the context of person-centered therapy. Rogers illustrates this open-mindedness on the subject of nonverbal communication and movement exercises in encounter groups, by including a dialogue he had with his daughter, Natalie, and his granddaughter, Anne. He included their comments, which reflected that Natalie was much freer than he was in employing both movement and contact in the groups she ran. He stated, "So both encounter groups, and the times, are changing," (Rogers, 1970, p.65).

Natalie Rogers established The Person–Centered Expressive Therapy Institute, in Santa Rosa, California, where she has integrated movement, art, and music into her groups. She wrote *The Creative Connection: The Expressive Arts as Healing* (N. Rogers, 1993).

Rollo May, Abraham Maslow, and James Bugental have all written at some length about the importance of creativity, both in life, and in the conceptualizations of humanistic psychology. The five basic postulates of humanistic psychology, which appear monthly at the front of *The Journal of Humanistic Psychology*, include this statement: "Human beings are intentional, are aware that they cause future events, and seek meaning, value, and creativity" (Greening, 2001, p.3).

Carl Rogers, an outstanding member of the founding group of humanistic psychologists, was also very interested in many aspects of creativity. In 1957, he wrote about creativity as a part of "A Therapist's View of the Good Life," for the journal, *The Humanist*. This article was later integrated into *On Becoming A Person* (Rogers, 1961). However, the section on creativity remained unchanged:

> A person who is involved in the directional process which I have termed 'the good life' is a creative person....He would be the type of person from whom creative products and creative living emerge....He would live constructively, in as much harmony with his culture as a balanced satisfaction of needs demanded.
>
> He would be able creatively to make sound adjustments to new as well as old conditions. (pp.193-194)

Rogers' definition of the word creativity in these examples was focused upon the ways in which a life is lived. A creative life must be adaptive to a person's contemporary culture, with an essential caveat. Rogers referred to a "balanced satisfaction of needs," which refers to a personal set of individualized needs, rather than a generalized adaptation to the demands of society. He also recognized the changing nature of a person's need to adjust as life's conditions change and evolve.

Rogers (1961) expanded these ideas in "Toward a Theory of Creativity," which also appeared in *On Becoming a Person*, 1961. His definition of the creative process was rich and expansive: "The creative process…is the emergence in action of a novel relational product, growing out of the uniqueness of the individual on the one hand, and the material, events, people or circumstances of his life on the other" (Rogers, 1961, p.350).

Rogers' definition included all four aspects of creativity that were formulated in Ross Mooney's (1963) paper, "A Conceptual Model for Integrating Four Approaches to The Identification of Creative Talent," (Mooney, 1963). Mooney's four approaches were to study either the creative environment, the creative product, the creative process, or the creative person (p.332).

Rogers also specified that creativity can be displayed in many ways, which M. A. Runco and R. Richards (1997) designated as the difference between eminent creativity and everyday creativity.

Rogers (1961) continued his discussion of creativity by highlighting the motivation for the creative process which is "man's tendency to actualize himself, to become his potentialities" (p.351). Rogers thought that the process of actualization was similar to the psychotherapeutic process that involved "the nature of the human species to live constructively" (p.353).

In developing his theory of creativity, Rogers (1961) explored many aspects of creativity, such as "The creative process, the motivation for creativity, the inner conditions of constructive creativity, the creative act and its concomitants and the conditions required to foster constructive creativity" (pp.347-359).

Rogers (1961) specified that he organized his ideas in this specific fashion for the purpose of research, and he hoped that rigorous testing would ensue, since he thought that is was necessary for human beings to develop "creative behavior in adapting ourselves to our new world if we are to survive" (p.359). Ross Mooney, Ruth Richards and others have expanded upon Rogers' ideas about creativity, and the research he envisioned did take place in later years.

Perhaps Carl Rogers was to serve as the best example of his views on creativity. His contribution of person-centered psychotherapy found many advocates throughout the United States and the rest of the world, and his ideas were applied in a variety of fields. His early book, *Counseling and Psychotherapy: Newer Concepts in Practice* (1942), focused upon the needs of children and their parents (individually and together), and he developed a specific set of techniques to be utilized. The introduction of this book included a statement that reflected Rogers' positive, humanistic viewpoint: "We have too little, rather than too much, faith in the growth capacities of the individual" (p.ix).

Rogers' professional work began in the fields of counseling and individual psychotherapy. However, "the person-centered approach exerted a significant influence on education, medicine, business, social work, the ministry, and numerous other professions" (Kirschenbaum & Henderson, 1989, p. 433). This expansion of the Rogerian influence occurred because Rogers continued to explore, and to ask important questions about his own work. For example, he inquired,

> Does a person-centered approach have anything to offer in solving these immense and dangerous global issues?...Some of the basic *principles* have a coherence, a consistency, and a demonstrated effectiveness that deserve scrutiny. Many of these underlying principles involve the person-centered approach to the problem of power, control, and decision-making. (Rogers, 1977, pp.116-118)

Rogers took these ideas into the larger world and began to travel extensively, applying his ideas to a wide range of national and international conflicts.

In the last decade of his life, Rogers facilitated groups in the following countries in addition to the United States: Japan, Mexico, Venezuela, Brazil, Austria, Hungary, Poland, France, Switzerland, Germany, Finland, Italy, Spain, the Soviet Union, England, Ireland, and South Africa (Kirschenbaum & Henderson, 1989, pp.433-434). This expansion of his original, person-centered approach to psychotherapy into a global approach to international conflict, and into many fields of endeavor, was Rogers' most concrete example of what creativity truly means.

This portion of the literature review confirms that Carl Rogers rarely wrote about bodily movement during therapy sessions, although he reflected a willingness to listen to the ideas of others in this matter. He never overtly discussed dance, dancing, or dance therapy in his extensive writings. However, he was very much interested in creativity, and in having his ideas researched rigorously, and he served as an excellent example of the creative expansion and extension of his own ideas and theories.

James Bugental. James F. T. Bugental is the fourth of the founders of humanistic psychology to be discussed in this survey. He was born in 1915 and continues to be professionally active. In 1999, he published *Psychotherapy Isn't What You Think.* In 2001, *The Handbook of Humanistic Psychology: Leading Edges in theory, Research, and Practice* was published, and Bugental was one of its three editors. Maslow, May, and Rogers all continued to work professionally until they died, as did the dancers in this study.

As the youngest member of the quartet of humanistic psychology pioneers, Bugental's ideas were influenced by Abraham Maslow, Carl Rogers, and Rollo May. However, May had the most impact upon Bugental as he was developing his ideas and his theories. "In *Existence,* May spoke my language" (deCarvalho, 1991, p.64).

In 1997, I interviewed Bugental to discuss his view about the ways in which the neo-Freudians had influenced his evolving ideas. He spoke with me at great length, and with great patience, but he also challenged me to think more deeply about my own professional work. When I started to formulate ideas for my research, I approached him once again. This second time I asked him about any connections he might have had with dancers or dance therapists, hoping that I might examine how his ideas had affected them.

Bugental raised the issue of confidentiality with me, and then reminded me that he was no longer in private practice. He shared with me how much he and his wife enjoyed Michael Smuin's San Francisco Ballet Company. When I reviewed this conversation with Tom Greening (dissertation chair), he suggested that I contact Elizabeth Bugental, because she had been the Chairman of the Theater Arts Department at Immaculate Heart College. Elizabeth Bugental took the time to contact many of her former colleagues, but reported that she was unable to be very helpful. However, she sent an e-mail stating that she thought that

> Moving from theater into therapy was a natural progression for me, and I still think the arts are the best preparations for good therapeutic work. There are many reasons for this such as attention to the person including the body, and the focus upon process rather than content. My husband agrees with me about this. (E. Bugental, personal communication, March 21, 2000)

This e-mail was extremely encouraging, and I anticipated that Bugental's writing would reveal his interest in the arts and the importance of bodily movement (such as dance or dance therapy). The literature review revealed that Bugental had written very little on these subjects. However, when he wrote *The Search for Authenticity,* Bugental (1965/1981) devoted a chapter to "Beyond The Human Frontier" in which he discussed the importance of the arts and creativity.

Bugental stressed the significance of humanity's search for awareness, and the need to experience the whole of existence. He stated that one should not artificially separate art from science, because

> The purest science is the most artistic....The arts in all the manifold forms—are essential to man's very humanity. That life is less than human in which there is no place for form, color, grace, composition, harmony, and contrast. Fantasy, melody, movement, and inspiration are the very

stuff of our most authentic being. (p.410)

This very strong statement captured Bugental's viewpoint about the importance of the creative arts. In this profoundly philosophical book, Bugental's assertion mandates an involvement in, and a response to, the arts as an essential part of a person's progression toward wholeness and authenticity.

Bugental expanded these ideas further as he contemplated the "Conditions of Being Human," (1965/1981, pp. 442-448). He examined these conditions meticulously, and decided that *Embodiedness* needed to be included as one of these existential givens, because

> As beingness is manifested on the objective plane, the physical body is its vehicle and sets its limits. Our bodies are the always-present condition of our conscious experience, so that the fact of embodiedness permeates all phases of our living. (p.443)

This is the strongest statement made by any of the four humanistic psychology pioneers about the primacy of bodily experiences. Bugental expanded upon this by applying his criteria of "necessary existential conditions" to the dimension of embodiedness. The first of these conditions is the confrontation with change, and the human body is the perfect example of a person's ever-changing existence. The body grows, changes, expands and contracts, becomes stronger then weaker, and eventually declines and dies. The human body, and our embodied selves, are graphic illustrations of a human being's continual change (and of our potential for development as well as decay).

Existential anxiety is another aspect of our human condition, and the human body provides a template upon which our anxieties are written. The experience of physical pain initially comes upon us as a surprise and intrudes upon our consciousness. Severe pain can drown out our awareness of other aspects of life, and our anxiety about pain "is a forerunner of destruction, the absolute" (Bugental, 1965/ 1981, p. 444). Bugental specified that this type of destruction meant an irretrievable loss, such as the loss of a beloved pet, or friend, or family member, or even the loss of our possessions or personal possibilities.

These kinds of embodied pain and destruction are early teachers about existential anxiety. We cannot be shielded from all of the occurrences, so we learn to be anxious about them: we experience this fear within our bodies. Existential dread may be expressed in bodily illnesses, such as anorexia nervosa, "tension headaches," and ulcers. The psychogenic origin of these illnesses has been debated throughout the literature (e.g., Bruch, 1973, pp.44-65; Frank & Frank, 1991, pp. 113-131; Luzzatto, 1995, pp. 60-75; Schwartz & Kline, 1997, pp.177-193; Stark, Aronow, & McGeehan, 1989, pp.121-143).

Bugental added existential joy to his list of the conditions of being, and wrote about what occurs when this condition is combined with being embodied.

> When we are fully in our healthy bodies and experiencing them, we find the existential joy of *movement*, of feeling ourselves using our structures-whether in sports, in dance, in love-making, in walking, restful sleep. The sense of *vitality* that emerges from this way of being is a rich one....It can be known at any age when we take the responsibility and opportunity to accept and fulfill our embodiedness. (Bugental, 1965/1981, p.446)

Therefore, embodiedness becomes an essential condition for being human, according to Bugental's criteria, because, when combined with existential joy, it provides us all with both movement and vitality. Bugental stressed our personal responsibility to accept that we are fully embodied human beings, not merely thinkers or doers. And he believed that we have an obligation to ourselves to explore and uphold our state of being embodied persons.

Bugental also emphasized the need for personal courage among his conditions for being human. He believed that if one employs courage to meet whatever our personal conditions of physical being, we might experience *wholeness*, which is defined as the physical aspect of authenticity. Bugental summarized his ideas in this way: "Full living calls for a quality of being in one's body and one's experiencing...*spiritedness*....This is an expression of vital, aware, and courageous participation in being" (Bugental, 1965/1981, p.444).

Bugental's statements about the importance of the concept of embodiment, and its place within his existential humanistic viewpoint are exceptionally clear. However, it is a source of profound disappointment to this researcher that Bugental did not expound further upon these theories. His many subsequent books have been focused upon the art of psychotherapy (and the art of being a psychotherapist), and upon extended explorations of the psychotherapeutic process. His books are filled with discussions of his particular approach to intensive psychotherapy. He has enriched these books with case histories, and extensive discussions of the process, the feelings and concerns of the psychotherapist, and the results of his work as a therapist and teacher. These books provide a psychotherapeutic practitioner with many ideas, as well as challenges to established practices and beliefs. However, Bugental did not expand upon his creative ideas about the importance of embodiment within the entire lifespan, nor within the therapeutic milieu.

The Dancers: Historical Introduction and Literature Review

This review of the dancers focuses upon those who have specifically contributed to the growth and development of American modern dance. The dancers surveyed are Ted Shawn, Ruth St. Denis, Mary Wigman, Martha Graham, and Hanya Holm. Shawn, St. Denis, and Wigman represent the first generation of modern dancers. Mary Wigman has been included because she embodies the German Expressionist dance that evolved after World War I and had such a profound impact upon the growth of American modern dance. The ideas and the work of Wigman played the same role in the growth of American dance as the Neo-Freudians played in the development of humanistic psychology (Hoffman, 1999b).

The second generation of American modern dancers is represented here by

Martha Graham and Hanya Holm. These two dancers were selected for review because they are the dance teachers most often cited by the research participants as their most important dance teachers. (See Table 1, pp.183-184.)

Several additional members of the second generation of modern dancers were invited to participate in this study, but they elected not to do so. They include Merce Cunningham, Paul Taylor, and Jim May (collaborator with Anna Sokolow). The 10 dancers who joined this study are considered (McDonagh, 1976) to be the third generation of American modern dancers. Their stories are told in their own words in the interviews. A portion of each interview includes relevant material on their teachers, where the teachers studied, and other historical material.

Ted Shawn. Ted Shawn (1891-1972) represents a major force in the development of American modern dance. His contributions to this evolutionary process have three major components, which can be framed chronologically. From 1915 to 1930, Shawn and Ruth St. Denis created the Denishawn schools, the *Denishawn Magazine*, and the Denishawn dancers. The Denishawn dancers performed all over the world, touring throughout the United States, Europe, and Asia. They carried the Denishawn vision of dance to a vast new audience (Poindexter, 1963).

Ted Shawn purchased Jacob's Pillow in 1931, beginning the second phase of his life's work. The era of the Men Dancers spanned 1933 to 1940. During this time, Shawn recruited and trained a group of men (originally nondancers), who lived with him at Jacob's Pillow. Shawn then choreographed a series of dances specifically designed for his new touring group, the Men Dancers. This troop introduced the first all-male dance company in the world. This period of time also marked the beginning of the Jacob's Pillow Dance Festival.

The final phase of Shawn's career spanned the years 1940 until his death in 1972. During this time, Shawn developed the University of the Dance, a summer training facility for dancers, that was one of the first in the United States.

Ted Shawn was born in 1891. He had originally planned to become a

Methodist minister, but during his junior year in college, he contracted diphtheria. The medication that saved his life left him paralyzed from the waist down (Terry, 1976, pp.35-39).

During the period of his convalescence, Shawn was urged to study ballet "as therapy for his paralyzed muscles, and Shawn began ballet lessons with Hazel Wallack, an accomplished dancer and teacher" (Maynard, 1965, p.86). Shawn also began to attend a variety of dance performances in Denver. He saw the Russian dancers such as Anna Pavlova, he saw the students of Isadora Duncan, and in 1911 he first saw Ruth St. Denis. St. Denis's performance was a revelation for Shawn and "proved to him that dance was a sacred art" (Poindexter, 1963, p.129). His previous background as a potential minister made his alert to the "broad possibilities of dance for religious worship, as church dance" (Maynard, 1965, p.87). Shawn pursued this particular interest of his for many years, and wrote about it in several contexts.

In 1960, Shawn reflected,

> I gave the first Christian church service in dance forms more than forty years ago....Since 1950 I have given a number of religious dance lectures to church groups, and in Boston I taught and conducted roundtable discussions at a three-day meeting of leaders of religious rhythmic choirs from all over New England. From that conference grew an organization designed to correlate the activities of groups interested in sacred dance....A Rhythmic Choir course, first given at the Pillow in 1958...is now an annual pre-season event. (Shawn, 1960, p.284)

There were three institutes of the Sacred Dance Guild that were held at Jacob's Pillow in early summer during the years 1959, 1960 and 1961 (Poindexter, 1963, p. 353). Research Participant #1 was involved in these institutes.

By 1912, Ted Shawn had moved to Los Angeles. This was the era of ballroom dancing, and when Shawn opened his dancing school, he felt obliged to teach such dances as "The Bunny Hug," "The Turkey Trot," and "The Texas Tommy" (Poindexter, 1963, p.133). Shawn also attempted to learn more about dance by attending vaudeville, early motion pictures, and performances of travelling dance companies. Whatever Ted Shawn learned about the nature of dance, he incorporated into his dance classes, and taught to his students. There is an advertisement from this era that demonstrates the range of dance that Shawn offered at his dance studio in 1912. The leaflet advertised that Shawn (and his colleague, Norma Gould) were teaching classes in the following:

> Grecian, Oriental, Nature and Barefoot, Rhythmics and Aesthetics, Choreographic Drama, Dance Pantomime, Music Interpretation, Dance Originating Instruction and Training in National and Folk Dance, Ballet Dancing, Step Dances, Advanced and Fancy Ball-room Dancing. (Gould & Shawn, 1912, advertisement)

The scope and diversity of the classes offered at this studio is an important indication of Shawn's thinking about the nature of dance. He was to expand upon these ideas throughout his career, incorporating them into the Denishawn repertory, the choreography of the Men Dancers, and the curriculum of the University of the Dance at Jacob's Pillow.

Shawn went to New York City in 1914 to study the varieties of dance, and to study with Ruth St. Denis (whom he had seen in performance in Los Angeles). She invited him first to audition for her, then to join her touring group of dancers, and finally to become her leading man, and dancing partner (Poindexter, 1963, p.151).

Ted Shawn and Ruth St. Denis were married on August 13, 1914, beginning the Denishawn era, which lasted until 1930. St. Denis and Shawn separated at that time, but never divorced. The Denishawn era was highly significant in the history of American modern dance. Denishawn embodied two important ideas: there were the Denishawn Dance Schools, which taught many different styles of dance, and the Denishawn Dancers, who toured throughout the United States, Europe, and Asia. These dancers presented the newest ideas in American dance to many thousands of people who had never seen dance before. By 1927, there were Denishawn schools in Los Angles, New York City, Rochester, Boston, Wichita, Minneapolis, and Westport (Poindexter, 1963, p. 160). Marian Chace, a Denishawn dancer who became the "mother" of dance/movement therapy, opened a Denishawn school in Washington, D.C., in the 1930s (Hoffman, 1999c).

When Shawn opened the Denishawn school in New York City in 1922, he was assisted by Martha Graham (who had been a Denishawn student and teacher in Los Angeles), and Louis Horst (an accompanist and musician; Poindexter, 1963, p.169).

It is important to be aware that while the Denishawn schools were being established through the United States, the Denishawn dancers were traveling throughout the United States, Europe, and the Orient (Schlundt, 1962).

The Denishawn organization had a tremendous impact upon American modern dance, and has been cited as "the cradle and stronghold of modern dance in America" (Maynard, 1965, p.94). Denishawn introduced new ideas and forms in dance to a vast audience of people throughout the world. Denishawn integrated classical literature, mythology, ethnic styles, and religious themes into the world of dance, changing the form forever. This was the beginning of American modern dance.

Three Denishawn students, Martha Graham, Doris Humphrey, and Charles Weidman, departed from Denishawn in the 1920s. Martha Graham left Denishawn in 1923 to follow her own path, and Louis Horst left two years later (1925). Shortly thereafter, Humphrey and Weidman also went out on their own. Horst had been Denishawn's musical director, and Graham, Humphrey, and Weidman were three of the school's most valuable assets. Horst went on to become Graham's mentor (and her lover), and became famous as a teacher of compositional forms of dance. Graham, Humphrey, and Weidman became three notable members of the second generation of American modern dancers (Terry, 1976, pp.120-121). By 1930, Ruth St. Denis and Ted Shawn had separated, and the Denishawn schools and touring company had been dissolved. The final performances of Denishawn were held at Lewisohn Stadium in New York City in 1931 (Schlundt, 1962).

Ted Shawn purchased Jacob's Pillow in 1931, beginning the second and third major phases of his professional career. He described seeing the property:

> Its house, which had been closed for five years, was in disrepair, and the grounds were overgrown but on sight I loved the land. I sold my Japanese pavillion at Westport, and bought the place near Lee, Massachusetts, that was to become famous as my summer school and dance theater. In the house I found letterheads that read "Jacob's Pillow, a Mountain Farm— Arthur E. Morgan, Prop." (Shawn, 1960, p.227)

This scenic site was also of historical importance in Massachusetts. Jacob's Ladder Trail was originally part of the first network of roads built in Massachusetts. It was built in 1800 and was known as the Eighth and Tenth Massachusetts Turnpike. The trail was so named by the local community in response to its winding path. The local religious communities felt that these roads resembled the ladder upon which the Biblical Jacob (Genesis 28:11-12) had observed angels climbing into heaven. A large rock that was found at the summit was named Jacob's Pillow.

The George Carter Farm, dating from 1790, was the original name of the site that became the Jacob's Pillow Dance Festival. Carter was an abolitionist, and during the Civil War the farm became a stop on the Underground Railway. During this period, the Carter family housed many runaway slaves from the Southern states, as they traveled north to upstate New York and Canada (Jacob's

Ladder Trail, Mobile Exhibition, Jacob's Pillow, 2001).

This historical site was to become Ted Shawn's home base for the remainder of his life. He began to pursue one of his fondest dreams, which was to develop an all male dance company. During 1931-1932, Shawn presented a short program featuring three male dancers. This led to a teaching job at Springfield College, in the physical education department. Shawn (1960) described how he taught his recalcitrant students:

> I gave them my alphabets of indivisible units of movement, and then, by combining these, spelled out words in motion, without ever using French ballet terms....
>
> These we worked into dances; rowing a boat; working with tools like the ax and the two-man saw; or scything a field. I used simple Negro spirituals for music that the students loved....With the sympathetic music of spirituals, strong and rhythmic, the students found themselves at home, and danced with gusto and surprising effectiveness. (p.243)

These ideas, so simply expressed, became the basis for the choreography of the Men Dancers. On March 21, 1933, Ted Shawn presented a full 2- hour program, devoted to dances that had been choreographed for and performed by men dancers. The positive response by the Boston audience and critics encouraged Shawn to move ahead with his plans for a professional men's group.

The six original members of the Men Dancers, an accompanist-composer, and Ted Shawn himself took up residence at Jacob's Pillow in 1933. They faced tremendous challenges: not only did the men have to study dance, learn new programs and create their own costumes, but they also had to raise the food they ate, cut firewood, and build the houses in which they lived at The Pillow. "Each member of the Men's Group built his own cabin, and the group as a whole built a kitchen and dining room adjoining the main house" (Poindexter, 1963, p.292).

Many of the original cabins are still in use, and one of the research participants in this study mentioned with pride that he had stayed in one of these cabins.

The Men Dancers continued until 1940, touring during the fall, winter, and spring. During the summers, the Men Dancers were in residence at Jacob's Pillow. There were weekly lecture–demonstrations, at which tea and sandwiches were served to the audiences. The men made and served the food, parked the cars, and then participated in Shawn's lecture-demonstrations. "Between 1933 and 1940, Shawn and the Men's Group had presented over 1,250 performances in over 750 cities in the United States, Canada and England" (Poindexter, 1963, p.284).

It was during this time that Shawn opened a summer school of dance. Originally, only men were accepted into the school as resident students. In 1938, a class was started for women teachers and "advanced girl students with arrangements for them to live at Greenwater Lodge near Jacob's Pillow" (Poindexter, 1963, p.251). Carol Lynn, a former Denishawn student, initiated these classes. Ted Shawn was convinced to teach afternoon classes for the new group of women. These classes represented the beginning of the University of the Dance, which is held each summer in conjunction with the Jacob's Pillow Dance Festival.

By 1940, the Men Dancers had disbanded, and Shawn was ready to focus upon the development of the University of the Dance. Shawn (1960) stated, "Since the final performance of my men's group...I have worked ceaselessly in the field of dance education, a new career, my third, as challenging to me as the first two" (p.277).

Ted Shawn had been a tireless advocate for incorporating dance into the educational system. In 1938, he delivered a series of lectures to a group of teachers in Nashville, Tennessee. In one of these lectures, he spoke about the benefits of dance upon the personality and its level of health.

The next [generation] should be a generation that has moved rhythmically and expressively from babyhood, so that each is a spontaneous unity....The bodies of all of them must be free and elastic, so that words and movement come forth as a two stream—and this will have, as an important offshoot, the production of a far more emotionally sound personality than is the rule today. A life of training in the dance...should have so produced a mental and emotional hygiene that there will be no antisocial behavior and no inhibited emotions to cause disruption in the psyche...so that when he arrives at adult status he will have something to contribute to the stream of human culture instead of being a problem and a drain on the public purse. (Shawn, 1940, p.80)

This statement reflects Shawn's firm conviction about the importance of dance movement to emotional health and stability. He was, first and foremost, a tireless teacher and advocate during all of the phases of his life. Marian Chace, a Denishawn student and dancer, who went on to establish the field of dance therapy, was the first to demonstrate the efficacy of Shawn words in her work at St. Elizabeth's Hospital during the 1940s (Hoffman, 1999c).

In 1940, Ted Shawn attempted to sell Jacob's Pillow but found no buyers. It was leased instead to Mary Washington Ball, who initiated "The Berkshire Hills Dance Festival" with a total of nine programs. These programs contained ballet, modern, and Spanish dance performances. This diverse programming was to become a feature of the subsequent Jacob's Pillow Dance Festivals (Owen, 1997a, p. 65).

In 1941, Shawn leased Jacob's Pillow once again, this time to a patron of Alicia Markova and Anton Dolin (English ballet stars). A series of programs were scheduled, and a school of dance was established. Ted Shawn was a teacher in this new school. The first summer program was called the "International Dance Festival," and it featured the following performers: Ruth St. Denis, Ted Shawn, Alicia Markova, Anton Dolin, Irina Baronova, Seiko Sarnia, Barton Mumaw, Paul Draper, Agnes deMille, and members of the Ballet Theater Company, such as Lucia Chase, Nora Kaye, and Antony Tudor (Shawn, 1947, pp. 20-24).

In 1942, a new Ted Shawn Theater opened at Jacob's Pillow, becoming the first theater in the United States built to meet the needs of dance performances. "The University of the Dance" also started officially at The Pillow in 1942, and featured such diverse teachers as Bronislava Nijinska, Joseph Pilates, and Ted Shawn (Owen, 1997a, p.66).

Each performance presented at Jacob's Pillow followed the original pattern established by Mary Washington Ball, mixing ballet, modern, and ethnic dance on each program. Many of the dancers also taught at The University of the Dance, providing the students with a depth and diversity of instruction that was rare. This pattern of programming lasted for the next 20 years (Owen, 1997a, p.23).

Another important aspect of the Jacob's Pillow programming has been the inclusion of many smaller professional dance companies from the United States, Canada, Europe, India, and other Asian countries.

After Ted Shawn's death in 1972, the programming pattern was changed, and dance companies were invited to perform for five days at a time. The diversity of The Pillow's programming is maintained in another manner. In addition to the Ted Shawn Theater, the Doris Duke Studio offers smaller (lesser known) companies the opportunity to perform. Finally, a new performance space, Inside Out, offers the newest young dance groups a performance venue. It is possible to spend a Saturday or Sunday at Jacob's Pillow and observe three companies in performance.

Ted Shawn's legacy to American dance has been extensive, and he has been deemed the "father" of American dance (Terry, 1976). As a co-leader of the Denishawn group, he developed the Denishawn schools and the Denishawn dancers, who toured throughout the world. He was a choreographer, performer, and tour leader during those years (1914-1930).

Shawn created the Men Dancers, a company that was unique and revolutionary in its era. Shawn was teacher, choreographer, and group leader during this time (1933-1940). In 1941, Ted Shawn turned his attention to dance education, and developed the Jacob's Pillow Dance Festival and the University of the Dance. Although The Pillow experienced many difficult years after Shawn's death in 1972, it currently appears to have attained a new level of financial stability, and has become a highly respected international dance center.

In 2001, Jacob's Pillow was designated as an American Irreplaceable Dance Treasure and was named to the National Register of Historic Places. In 2002, Jacob's Pillow celebrated its 70th Anniversary, a testament to the vision of Ted Shawn On May 27, 2003, Jacob's Pillow was designated a National Historic Landmark, the only dance venue to be so named.

One aspect of Shawn's life that has not been adequately documented, and is of interest to this investigator, is his knowledge of psychology, and the literature of this field. His biographer, Betty Poindexter (1963), stated that Shawn had "read ...many classic works of literature, and was thoroughly conversant with poetry, belle-lettres, history, religion and philosophy" (Poindexter, 1963, p.274). Ted Shawn wrote many books but did not offer substantive bibliographies or references for his ideas. In his biographical book, *One Thousand and One Night Stands*, Shawn (1960) recalled an encounter he had with a "British spinster-psychoanalyst doing graduate work....The distinctions [I made] were beyond the lady psychoanalyst who had pegged me her way and did her best to alter my ego" (p.224). This story is the only reference to psychoanalysis in Shawn's writings, but it does indicate a familiarity with the terminology of the field.

It was Agnes deMille, in her 1991 biography of Martha Graham, who offered the only concrete information about Ted Shawn's knowledge of psychology. In a description of the early Denishawn days in Los Angeles, deMille said, "Ted gave lectures on dance history, and read Walter Pater, Havelock Ellis, Freud, and Nietzsche aloud to the young men after class....He became the father leader, the alter ego, Papa Shawn' (p.49).

This quote provides the only evidence found that the highly literate Ted Shawn had any familiarity with the writings of Sigmund Freud. There is no evidence that Shawn read the work of the next generation, such as the neo-Freudians Clara Thompson, Harry Stack Sullivan, Karen Horney, Erich Fromm, or Frieda Fromm-Reichmann.

Ruth St. Denis. Ruth St. Denis is the second member of the first generation of modern dance pioneers. She was born in 1879, one year after Isadora Duncan. It is important to realize this chronological connection because these two women affected the world of dance in very different ways. Duncan, while "remaining an American 'character,' became a world artist who influenced the art-dance of Russia and Germany and England as much as or more than she did American dance" (Kendall, 1979, p.12).

Ruth St. Denis was acclaimed as the woman who began the lineage of American modern dance. She was to set many historical precedents, one of which emerged from the interviews in this study. St. Denis died in 1968, and she performed her celebrated dance, *Incense,* for the last time in 1966, when she was 87 years old (Shelton, 1981, p.269). It will be seen that the third generation of American modern dancers also does not retire from their professional careers, but continues to teach, choreograph, and even perform into the later years of their lives.

Emma Hull Dennis (mother of Ruth St. Denis) was an extraordinary woman for her era. She was born into an alcoholic, abusive family and was described as having a "chronic nervous condition" (Shelton, 1981, p.7). She was, however, the second woman to graduate from the University of Michigan Medical School. Medical education in this era was strongly influenced by Dr. Samuel Hahnemann, the founder of homeopathic medicine in the United States. Hahnemann's anti-allopathic message became an integral part of Emma Hull's belief system. Hull suffered a nervous collapse after graduation from medical school and spent a year at the Jackson Sanitarium in Danville, New York.

Dr. James C. Jackson, Director of the Sanitarium, had instituted a revolutionary regimen for his patients, who were labeled as "neurasthenic females." The women at the sanitarium were required to take hipbaths, exercise daily, and follow a strict diet; they were uncorseted, and wore short dresses. They were encouraged to revolt against the contemporary standards in women's clothing and to become interested in social reforms, such as women's rights.

Another aspect of Jackson's hospital program was known as therapeutic social dancing. This revolutionary idea was part of the regimen at the Sanitarium, because Jackson believed that social dancing allowed women two important opportunities: first, to participate in recreational situations with men; and second, to provide a balance between the emotional, physical, and spiritual aspects of an individual's life (Shelton, 1981, pp.3-5).

Emma Hull Dennis was to pass along many of these innovative ideas to her daughter, Ruth. On March 17, 1936, Ruth St. Denis delivered a lecture on the importance of dance education, and stated:

Dance education should be integrated into higher education and spiritual education.

It is not that we should specialize less, but that we should humanize more. Our disintegrations show in our bodies as well as our minds. What single act can polarize and focus the forces of life—physical, emotional and spiritual—like the dance? (St. Denis, 1997, p.86)

St. Denis was offering an extremely early description of the value of dance as a therapeutic modality, adding her own spiritual framework. We also note her use of the word "humanize," which she employed to mean a therapy that serves to integrate the mind, body, and spirit. These ideas were advanced for their time (1936), and heralded ideas that were to evolve during the 1950s and 1960s.

Emma Dennis had also become interested in the Delsarte System, which was based upon the teachings of Francois Delsarte. In this system, the

"Law of correspondences"...assigned a metaphysical equivalent to each physical act....Bodily movement [was divided] into three great orders:

oppositional movement, with body parts moving in opposite directions simultaneously to express force and power; parallel movement, with body parts moving simultaneously in the same direction, denoting physical weakness; and successive movements which pass through the entire body, expressive of emotion. (Stebbins, 1902, p.67)

The Delsarte System was adopted enthusiastically in the United States in the 1870s and 1880s. Genevieve Stebbins, developed a series of exercises, which became the basis of Ruth St. Denis' original dance training.

The Dennis family was continually struggling financially and Emma Dennis hoped that her daughter, Ruth, might become a contributor. She encouraged Ruth to become a dancer, and took her to many auditions (Shelton, 1981).

In 1892, Emma Dennis took her 13-year-old daughter to a "Delsarte Matinee given on behalf of the National Christian League for the benefit of the Social Party at the Madison Square Theatre" (Shelton, 1981, p.13). The artist was Genevieve Stebbins, and her performance was later described by Ruth St. Denis as "the real birth of my art life" (St. Denis, 1939, p.16).

Historically, the Stebbins' Delsarte exercises introduced a variety of movements that contemporary Americans consider to be modern dance. Stebbins utilized oppositional arm swings, a trunk that could bend forward and backwards, subtle shifts of weight, and backfalls to the floor. All of these exercises were activated by the rhythms of the breath as it contracts and relaxes.

The importance of Stebbins' method as a basis for modern technique was its energizing of neglected areas of the body—the torso, arms, sides, and head—and its creative placement of the body in space, use of varying levels from lying to kneeling to standing, and its built-in dynamic based on breath motivation. (Shelton, 1981, p.15)

Ruth St. Denis began her dancing career as a dancer in vaudeville when she was 15. She became "skirt dancer," a title that had also been applied to Isadora Duncan.

The skirt dancers combined the balance and the pirouettes of the ballet style, added the gracefulness of the flowing drapery, the simplicity and naturalness of the Greek dance, added a touch of acrobatics, and went into vaudeville, where they were welcomed as novelty numbers (Flitch, 1912, p.71).

In 1900, Ruth Dennis met David Belasco, who was to change her life, as well as her name to Ruth St. Denis. She toured with his company to England and then traveled across the country with his play, *Zaza*. She continued working with him until 1905.

In 1904, in Buffalo, New York, Ruth St. Denis noticed a poster for Egyptian cigarettes in a drugstore window. St. Denis (1939) said that she knew "That my destiny as a dancer had sprung alive in that moment. I would become a rhythmic and impersonal instrument of spiritual revelation rather than a personal actress of comedy or tragedy" (p.52).

St. Denis had become a Christian Scientist the previous summer, which became an integral part of her life, and served as a focus for her evolving interest in mysticism (Shelton, 1981, p.47). The next few years were extremely productive. She began to research Egyptian and Indian mythology, seeking to uncover the background of the dances that were her particular legacy to modern dance.

On March 22, 1906, Ruth St. Denis presented three dances, *Radha, Incense,* and *The Cobras.* The renowned dance critic, Jack Anderson, discussed the importance of St. Denis' performance:

> Each [dance] was visually arresting. *Radha* and *Incense* also attempted to cloak spiritual messages in exotic trappings....In *The Cobras*...St. Denis portrayed a snake charmer....As she twisted her long arms, the [emerald] rings resembled snakes' eyes while her arms became serpents slithering

and writhing about her neck and body....*The Cobras* was also a kinetic experiment. Lacking fancy kicks and turns, it employed only a few carefully chosen movements. (Anderson, 1997, p.37)

This program was to catapult St. Denis' career into new arenas. She gathered sponsors and support and began to tour. She went to Europe, performing in London, Paris, Vienna, Rome, and many cities in Germany. After she had danced for the Weimar court, "The German government offered to build a theater as the foundation for St. Denis' art philosophy, and to give her a home and a pension for life if she would remain in Germany" (Maynard, 1965, p.83).

However appealing this offer might have been, Ruth St. Denis returned to the United States in 1909, with her personal wealth and her reputation established (Shelton, 1981, pp.67-87).

For the next six years, Ruth St. Denis toured the United States, sometimes as a solo performer, other times as a star in a vaudeville performance. In 1912, the American pubic took up social dancing, engaging in the "Turkey-trot," the "Bunny Hug," the "Tango," and the "Cakewalk." St. Denis found that she needed to include popular dances on her programs, and in order to do that, she needed a partner. In 1914, she auditioned a likely candidate, Ted Shawn, who became her dancing partner, and they were married that same year. At the time of their marriage, Shawn was 23 and St. Denis was 15 years his senior (Kendall, 1979, pp.93-113).

Their marriage continued until 1931, when they separated. St. Denis and Shawn never divorced, and they celebrated their 50th wedding anniversary with a gala performance at Jacob's Pillow, dancing together once again.

The history of the Denishawn Company, the schools, and the touring programs was discussed in the section on Ted Shawn. Although Shawn functioned as the director, financial manager, and organizer, St. Denis continued to work as a star performer, choreographer, and teacher for the Denishawn students.

When the Denishawn empire was dissolved, both Ruth St. Denis and Ted Shawn were faced with an accumulation of unpaid bills. Shawn had always taken care of the financial responsibilities, but the depression had undermined the prospects for performers of all kinds. Shawn was able to regroup financially, and subsequently purchased Jacob's Pillow, and began his work with the Men Dancers.

Ruth St. Denis struggled with finances for the rest of her life. In 1935, she needed to accept welfare to pay her rent. Shawn helped her financially whenever it was possible. St. Denis accepted whatever bookings she could and danced whenever possible. She refocused her work, and devoted her time to the development of her Society of Spiritual Arts and a Church of Divine Dance. She originated a Rhythmic Choir, which was to form the basis of her choreography.

In 1934, St. Denis choreographed the *Masque of Mary,* a ritual pageant designed for church presentation. This piece was first presented during the Christmas season at the Rutgers Presbyterian Church in New York City. The *Masque of Mary* was next presented at The Riverside Church, to more than 1700 worshipers. "Ruth had established a new stage personna, the Madonna, and a new era in her career" (Shelton, 1981, p.234).

The Rhythmic Choir continued to perform occasionally, but Ruth St. Denis also needed a steady income. In 1938, Dr. Paul Eddy, President of Adelphi College (in Garden City), offered St. Denis the opportunity to organize and direct a new dance department at Adelphi. Ruth St. Denis maintained this connection with Adelphi into the 1960s, stressing her "research into the dance as an instrument of religious worship" (Shelton, 1981, p.248). However, by then St. Denis had moved into new areas of her life.

In 1939, Ruth St. Denis completed her autobiography, *An Unfinished Life.* The publication of this book began a whole new era in St. Denis' career. Her Rhythmic Choir performed at the 1939 World's Fair in New York. In 1940, she was asked to perform and teach religious dance at Jacob's Pillow. When Ted Shawn invited her to return to The Pillow the following summer, St. Denis revived *Radha, Incense* and other solo dances.

Walter Terry (1941), the dance reviewer for *The New York Herald Tribune,* wrote, "Ruth St. Denis remains, in my estimation, the first lady of the American dance," (n.p.).

In December 1942, Ruth St. Denis moved to California, where she lived with her brother and sister-in-law for the rest of her life. However, she continued to work and to travel throughout the country. She took a job, briefly, at the Douglas Aircraft factory in Santa Monica, working on the "graveyard shift." She was then 64 years old.

Ted Shawn and "Miss Ruth" performed together again in April 1945, at a benefit performance for Jacob's Pillow. They were to perform together for the next 20 years. Shawn invited her up to Jacob's Pillow on a regular basis, where they danced together, argued, and fought to upstage each other. St. Denis had become a mythical figure at The Pillow, and was very much admired by the students.

On her 68th birthday, Ruth St. Denis formally launched her Church of Divine Dance. She spent her days teaching oriental and religious dance at the Pasadena Playhouse. She choreographed and performed a variety of Madonna ballets and continued to travel and to lecture. She never retired from her career, setting an example for the dancers who followed her.

In the last decade of her life, Ruth St. Denis received many awards that recognized her role in the history of American dance. She died in 1968, and was interred at Forest Lawn Cemetery. The marker on her vault contained one of her early poems (Shelton, 1981, pp.254-270).

> The Gods have meant
> That I should dance
> And in some mystic hour
> I shall move to unheard rhythms
> Of the cosmic orchestra of heaven

And you will know the language

Of my wordless poems

And will come to me.

For that is why I dance. (St. Denis, 1932, p.I)

Mary Wigman. American modern dance evolved as a reaction to the aesthetic rules of ballet and ethnic dance, arising from three distinct (and separate) streams. Ted Shawn believed in the widest parameters for dance and added the movements of farming, building, and everyday life to his choreography for the Men Dancers. Ruth St. Denis was drawn to the mystical and spiritual qualities that could be potentially expressed in dance. Shawn and St. Denis contributed their ideas through Denishawn.

The third stream of ideas in the evolutionary process of American modern dance came from Germany and was embodied by Mary Wigman.

Mary Wigman is the third member of the first generation of modern dancers to be discussed in this research study. She was born in 1886 and died in 1973. She is the only member of this group who was German rather than American born. However, the Wigman contributions to the development of modern dance represent essential elements of this evolving art form.

The features of German modern dance emerged in the teens and early twenties, out of the national enthusiasm for Physik-Kultur, the memories of Isadora Duncan's triumphs in Berlin and Munich, and the teachings of...Swiss-born Emile Jacques-Dalcroze. He believed that music education must be interpreted with movement. The systems of his student Rudolph Van Laban...who found out how to write dance down [Labanotation], describing and analyzing the various qualities, were also essential in the development of the new German dance. (Kendall, 1979, p.201).

Mary Wigman was the dancer who formed the connection between Dalcroze, and Laban, and created the new form of German modern dance. Wigman's students, such as Hanya Holm, and Harald Kreutzberg carried her ideas to America in the 1930s. German dance insisted upon self-discipline carried to the extremes, and "it put forth a philosophy of the Physical distilled until it became the spiritual" (Kendall, 1979, p.202).

In 1910, Wigman went to study with Jacques-Dalcroze in Hellerau, and she was offered a contract to run the Dalcroze School in Berlin in 1913. In the summer of 1913, Mary Wigman went to Ascona for the first time, upon the suggestion of her friend, the Expressionist painter, Emil Nolde. Ascona was an

> Idyllic center in the Southern Swiss Alps which around the turn of the century became a summer colony for artists and intellectuals. There, in 1913, Rudolph Laban, a Hungarian teacher, choreographer, and theorist, offered a summer dance course....Laban and his associates lived in huts, and when they were not studying or dancing, they did farm work, weaving and baking. (Anderson, 1997, p.49)

Ascona provided an environment similar to Jacob's Pillow in the 1930s. Ted Shawn and the men dancers lived in the houses they had to build, and they also had to raise their own food. The activities of construction and farming were actually incorporated into Shawn's choreographer for the men dancers.

Mary Wigman talked about Ascona that summer:

> In 1913 I made my first pilgrimage to that beautiful hill referred to as Monte Verita.... All I knew was that I was supposed to meet there the man of whom Emil Nolde had told me: "He moves as you do and dances as you do – without music." That was Rudolph Van Laban. He became my teacher. (Sorrell, 1973, p.26)

It was Rudolph Laban who challenged Mary Wigman to become a dancer, rather than a Dalcroze teacher. When Wigman showed Laban her contract to conduct the Dalcroze School in Berlin, he read it and responded,

> Well, I can only congratulate you on a beautiful and secure position for a lifetime....But what a pity. Actually you are a dancer who should be on stage....
>
> I did not sign the contract. I decided to remain free, even though I faced a frightening nothing. But even this nothingness was tempting and promising, full of artistic adventure. (Sorrell, 1973, p.27)

Laban was a rebel and a revolutionary innovator, and his direct encouragement led Mary Wigman to become another innovator, and a revolutionary in the field of modern dance. Wigman returned to Ascona to work with Laban in the summer of 1914, assisting him with his work on the "Harmony of Movement" (based upon the tension and relation of the body). Wigman's contribution was to demonstrate repeatedly movement combinations for Laban (Benbow-Niemier, 1998, p.824).

Wigman expressed her ambivalence about working with Laban so closely, and about her frustration, fatigue, and her lack of interest in the development of theory. However, she also understood something else about her work with Laban:

> I believe the foundation of my career as a dancer as well as a dance pedagogue were laid in those few weeks. Objectivity and responsibility, patience, endurance, and self-discipline. How I needed them when I worked on my solo program when my enthusiasm...for expression carried me away...What a struggle, what an inner fight....I had learned my lesson. I knew that, without killing the creative, I had to keep the balance between my emotional outburst and the merciless discipline of a super-personal control, thus submitting myself to the self-imposed law of dance

composition. (Sorrell, 1973, pp.39-40)

Mary Wigman was clearly searching for something original as she strove to develop a new form of dance. As one of the founders of modern dance, she had turned away from the forms of ballet, and from the essential formlessness of Isadora Duncan's interpretive dance. Nor did ethnic dance intrigue this pioneer. Louis Horst (1967), another pioneer in the field of modern dance, as a musician and choreography teacher, was to discuss this struggle:

> The pioneers in modern dance and their successors recaptured the relation that the primitive has to his body—an intimacy with the muscle tensions of daily movements which had been lost to modern men....It is, rather, an inner sensitivity to every one of the body's parts, to the power of its whole, and to the space in which it carves designs. (Horst & Russell, 1967, p.17)

As Wigman had elaborated, her quest was to discover some way to develop this sensitivity, and secondarily, to find a way to discipline the new form of movement, so that it could become a vehicle of communication. Martha Graham as well as Mary Wigman, began to choreograph in this innovative fashion, without the use of music. The original dances employed only natural sounds, such as stamping or clapping. Later, the use of percussion instruments was integrated into the dances. Both this form of dance and humanistic psychology stressed naturalness and authenticity.

This specific approach to music was different from the approach of Denishawn, and Duncan. Isadora Duncan, Denishawn, and later Ted Shawn and Ruth St. Denis, working as individual choreographers, all employed music as the basis of their dances. Wigman and Graham began with the movement, and explored the parameters of the movement, the use of space, and the rhythms that arose within the movement. Then they added music to accompany the original movement, or to be integrated into the movement patterns.

After World War I, Wigman was acclaimed by the German public both as a great dancer, and as an innovator. (Interview Participant #6 displayed a poster of Mary Wigman's first Berlin concert in 1919.) Wigman continued to strive during this time for the new forms that she sought in her dances. Horst and Russell (1967) made an interesting comparison between the development of German modern dance and the American form, in their discussion of the differences between Mary Wigman and Martha Graham.

> The Wigman dance, characteristic of German culture, was concerned with the relationship of man to his universe. Mary Wigman conceived of space as a factor, like time, with which to compose. The emphasis was thus taken off the body of the dancer and put onto the idea which the dancer wished to make manifest. The American Dancer, living in a new developing country, did not feel the enmity of limiting space, was less concerned with his use of it. His subject matter was chiefly an objective comment on his people and his times. (Horst & Russell, 1967, p.18)

It was Mary Wigman's training with Rudolph Laban that allowed her to understand space as a choreographic element. He had developed Labanotation, a recording system that displays the qualitative and quantitative aspects of movement, originally used in dance. Labanotation was developed further during World War II, to evaluate the movements of industrial worker in English factories, and was renamed Effort-Shape. The Effort-Shape Method of movement analysis explores such aspects of movement as Effort (how the body concentrates its exertions), Tension Flow (the energy moving between free flow and bound flow), Weight (the range of movement between lightness and strength), and Space (the use of space between the boundaries of direct and indirect; Dell, 1970).

Wigman devoted her early years as a dancer to the development of a dance technique, which did not yet exist and was for the "new dance." She wrote at some length about her journey of discovery:

> There was neither a model nor guidelines. There was only the novice, who, completely depending upon herself, entered on the most fascinating expedition for a dancer: to discover his own body and its metamorphosis from body into instrument....Time and again I gave myself up to the intoxification of this experience, to this almost lustful destruction of the physical being, a process in which, for seconds, I almost felt a oneness with the cosmos. (Sorrell, 1973, p.52)

Wigman's experiments were based upon the premise that the body needed to be turned into an instrument so flexible and fluid that it might express all varieties of emotion. It was therefore necessary to rediscover the body itself, and then to strengthen it physically, so that the body was capable of flowing into movement. To achieve these goals, Mary Wigman developed a new system of rhythmic exercises known as *Tanz Gymnastik*.

Wigman stated that her new form of gymnastics was embraced by the German people with joy. She believed that everyone could dance and might therefore discover, "stifled, half-formed emotions, and literally find a form of speech through the body" (Sorrell, 1973, p.53).

Mary Wigman (1973) was also an astute observer of her fellow Germans and was quick to note the impact of her work upon them. She felt that after World War I, the German population was

> ...growing up in a sad, discouraged world, a world that walked with its head hanging, its steps lagging....And they began to dance for the fun of it....Instead of dancing from a diagram of what other dancers have done before you, you travel the realms of the dance with your own body. (p.53)

Mary Wigman became the center of a national movement during the

1920s, one of many artists to flourish during the height of German Expressionism. She wrote with enthusiasm about the years in which German artists came into prominence:

> The stored up creative focus broke through. Everything seemed young and novel....Extreme contrasts collided, controversies were brought to a head, there was constantly a meeting of the minds....What all of these had in common was the wrestling for a personal message and its artistic expression of universality....I too was on the move and my pupils with me. (Sorrell, 1973, pp.54-55)

Wigman continued her reminiscence of the 1920s, discussing her interest in all of the arts and her friendship with such artists as Oskar Kokoschka, Paul Klee, Wassily Kandinsky, Lionel Feininger, Leon Kirschner, and Emil Nolde. She thus reflected the impact of the German zeitgeist upon the population of that era and the ways in which the artists interacted with each other. The Wigman contributions in the field of modern dance were an integral part of their time, carrying the energy of that stress-filled time for the German people.

The Wigman School in Dresden was established in 1920 and endured until 1943. Among her most famous pupils were Hanya Holm, Harald Kreutzberg, Gret Palucca, and Margharita Wallman (Sorrell, 1973, p.65). Holm, Kreutzberg, and Wallman were later responsible for bringing Wigman's work to the United States, Kreutzberg as a dancer, and Holm and Wallman as teachers.

In 1927, Wigman wrote an essay presenting her ideas about the importance of modern dance and the dancer's position during that evolutionary process. This essay was called "Stage Dance-Stage Dancer" and has been reprinted widely. It has been excerpted for use here.

> We find ourselves in a process of change as far as the dance is concerned: abandonment of the classical ballet in favor of an expression representing

our time. What are we looking for? To attune our inmost feelings to the mood of our time....

The confusion in the field of movement is great, and yet not so great as it may appear to the uninitiated. There may be many methods...but they all point to one purpose: to control the body for the body's sake. The ultimate and noblest meaning of the dance can have one aim only: the living work of art, presented through the body as its instrument of expression.

Hardly anyone of the gifted young people turning to the dance wants to become a ballet dancer...They all want to dance the way they feel, and the dancer's sensibility is...directed towards expressing the spirit of today's generation...They see in the dance a possibility to express their very being, they envision the stage as a place of artistic creation where they can develop their abilities and fight for new ideas...

Our dance is born of our age and our spirit, it has the stamp of our time as no other art form has. (Sorrell, 1973, pp.107-115)

The essence of German Expressionistic dance was most aptly described by its founder, Mary Wigman. Her words reflect the spirit of that time and explain the goals and aspirations of the dancers of that era.

Between the years of 1930 and 1933, Mary Wigman made three trips to America. During those three years, she performed a total of 170 times as she traveled throughout the United States. On her first two tours, she traveled with only her musical improviser-accompanist and her percussionist. In 1933, she traveled with her group of dancers. In an interview with *The New York Times* (November 18, 1932), Wigman discussed her battles with depression and how she dealt with these episodes.

To the artist, of course, even a depression is grist for the mill. But anybody can forget his troubles in rhythmic movement. It has always been my medicine, and I have had some tremendous depressions, quite private ones.

One never knows what inspires a creative work. I worked intensely on these dances, and when they were finished, I asked myself why they came out just so and not otherwise. I could not say why, but I had some of the same feeling as I had before the elemental power of America— something like the way I felt when I first saw Niagara Falls. (Sorrell, 1973, pp.152-153)

In these words, Wigman documented how her dancing had helped her to conquer the series of depressions that had been an integral part of her life. The use of expressive dance, utilized as a form of therapy, was undocumented at that time. Wigman's statement about the use of rhythmic movement was an insight of her own. This particular discovery was made once again by Marian Chace during the 1940s and 1950s, and became part of the literature of dance/movement therapy. Mary Wigman was an innovator in this aspect of her work as well.

In 1931, Hanya Holm (Wigman's pupil) opened the first Wigman School in the United States. It was fortunate that she did so, since Mary Wigman elected to remain in Germany during World War II. She died in West Berlin in 1973.

An interesting connection was made among members of the first generation of modern dance pioneers in 1930, when Ted Shawn performed in Germany and encountered German Expressionist dance. He spent several weeks rehearsing at the Wigman School in Berlin, working with Margarete Wallman. Shawn was so impressed with Wallman that he invited her to teach at Denishawn the next year. Wallman was also listed as a member of the faculty at Jacob's Pillow. However, Shawn was not impressed with the German version of modern dance, and he wrote:

German-modern dancing had no message for me personally, but in keeping with Denishawn's clearly stated dedication to every form of dance, I felt that our students should have firsthand knowledge of European dance developments.

Wigman's reputation already was influencing and intriguing dancers in America although neither she nor an authorized Wigman teacher had yet crossed the Atlantic. Wallman...through our school would be the first modern dancer of Germany to demonstrate and teach in the United States. (Shawn, 1960, pp.220-221)

After Shawn's acknowledgement of Wigman's reputation, he continued to discuss German modern dance, but denied the importance of her work and its originality.

Most of the *Collectif* [the German group in Berlin] had been influenced by Mary Wigman, and they kept telling me that certain dance developments and principles originated with her or with Rudolph Van Laban, her teacher. I often refuted their claims by showing them works in print, programs or pictures that we had done in America, frequently passing even beyond the discoveries attributes to the German-moderns. (Shawn, 1960, p.225)

Mary Wigman was the originator of the modern dance form that became known as German Expressionistic dance. Her ideas and her original work were transmitted to the United States on her tours, and later by her pupils Hanya Holm, Margarete Wallman, and Harald Kreutzberg. Her writings also documented the ways in which she employed her individualistic form of dance to assuage her depressions, making her one of the earliest dance therapists on record.

Her writings tell us nothing about her readings, so we cannot ascertain what she knew about the exciting new fields of psychology and psychoanalysis that were evolving in Germany and Switzerland during her most productive years.

Martha Graham. Martha Graham is the first of the two members of the second generation of modern dancers to be discussed in this study. She was one of the great revolutionaries of American modern dance. She was born in Allegheny, Pennsylvania in 1894 and died in 1991, at the age of 96. She choreographed 200 dances; and *Maple Leaf Rag* premiered in 1990, less than a year before her death (Campbell, 1999, pp.72-75). Graham's long involvement in her professional career is a characteristic of the dancers in this study.

Graham was selected for inclusion in this study for several reasons. First, Graham was a student of the Denishawn School in California and received her early dance training there. She taught in the Denishawn schools as well, and was an important member of the Denishawn Company. Her departure from Denishawn deeply offended Ted Shawn.

Another reason for Graham's inclusion in this study is that she developed an innovative dance technique, and her school and dance company became the training grounds for many generations of American modern dancers. It is not surprising that so many of the third generation of dancers (those interviewed in this study) listed Graham as one of their most important dance teachers.

Don McDonagh, in his diagram of "Extended Choreographic Families," listed Graham as the teacher and inspirational source for a diverse group of the third generation of dancers. This group includes Merce Cunningham, Viola Farber, Erick Hawkins, Anna Sokolow, Paul Taylor, Twyla Tharp, and James Waring (McDonagh, 1976, I, p.i).

In 1916, Martha Graham was 22. She attended a summer session at the newly opened Denishawn School in Los Angeles. Graham was enchanted by the beautiful Ruth St. Denis, and sought to study with her. St. Denis found Graham to be

> ...a short, unmalleable lump. She told Shawn that she couldn't do anything with Graham....So Shawn took over the teaching of Graham, Graham...improved so quickly under his guidance that St. Denis began to use her as a demonstrator in her own classes. (McDonagh, 1973, pp.22-23)

Soon Martha Graham was teaching at the Denishawn School. Ted Shawn went into the domestic Ambulance Corps during World War I. He invited Graham (and several other students) to live at the school and teach classes while he was away during the week. On weekends, Shawn returned to teach and to supervise the teachers. Graham continued to study and to teach at Denishawn, and she became a member of the Company, traveling with them on tours through the United States and Europe.

In 1921, Graham joined Shawn on a tour that was to change her life and to alter the landscape of the modern dance world. The touring group was very small: Shawn, Graham, Charles Weidman, Betty May, and Dorothea Bowen, and the group's music director, Louis Horst. It was during this tour that Martha Graham

> Became romantically attached to Louis Horst, a married man, ten years her senior....Their relationship, which began professionally, ripened into romance during the tour....The relationship between them struck deep roots [lasting] for twenty years. In the end, Horst was to have a singular effect on the whole history of modern dance. (McDonagh, 1973, p.31)

Horst was a professional musician, who began to accompany dance classes at the Denishawn School to supplement his income when his wife, Betty, began to study there. He became a personal and professional support to the young Martha Graham, "but the deepest attraction between them seemed to be in the realm of books and ideas" (Stodelle, 1984, p.36).

In 1921, Shawn's dancers appeared at the Apollo Theater on 42nd Street in New York City. The struggling group moved into the Chatsworth apartments on Riverside Drive, and became Denishawn East (McDonagh, 1973, p.32).

In 1923, Graham received an offer from "John Murray Anderson, designer and impresario, to dance in his chic Broadway revue, the Greenwich Village Follies" (Kendall, 1979, p.175). Graham took the opportunity to leave both Denishawn and her California home, and to begin a new life in New York City.

Martha Graham had outgrown the Denishawn Company, but Ted Shawn maintained a position of absolute authority. Graham asked permission to leave the company and,

> Miss Ruth claims she didn't care; Ted did, deeply, but he claims he bade her Godspeed....Ted was wounded to the heart, his pride shredded. In fact, Martha's defection caused part of Shawn's great bitterness and constituted the first wound in the flesh of the Denishawn Company. (deMille, 1991, p.68)

Graham's biographers have discussed the relationship between Graham and Shawn. McDonagh (1973) and deMille (1991) stress the enmity between these two, and they state that Graham was not invited to appear at Jacob's Pillow until 1984, 12 years after Shawn's death. In fact, Martha Graham attended the 1956 debut of the San Francisco Ballet at Jacob's Pillow. Her appearance led Shawn to write, "Martha loved our theatre, and gave me real hope that someday she will grace the stage of the Ted Shawn Theatre" (Owen, 2002, p.28).

Owen, The Pillow Archivist, recently discovered a significant piece of correspondence, dated January 9, 1957. This letter documents an earlier invitation from Shawn to Graham. This letter reads: "In 1942...when I knew that the theatre at Jacob's Pillow would definitely be finished for the summer season, Miss Graham was the very first artist invited to appear in the new theatre, and she accepted" (Shawn, 1957). In addition, a newly unearthed flyer from The Pillow archives reveals that Graham gave a lecture-demonstration at Jacob's Pillow in the summer of 1960. The flyer reads: "Ted Shawn, Founder-Director, Jacob's Pillow Dance Festival, has the honor to announce a special added event of extraordinary importance in the personal appearance of Martha Graham" (Shawn, 1960). Whatever bitterness Shawn may have felt towards his former pupil in 1923, had passed by the year 1942.

Graham's 1923 departure from Denishawn was only the first of several important defections. In 1925, Louis Horst left Denishawn to travel abroad. Shawn and St. Denis went on tour with the *Ziegfeld Follies*, leaving Doris Humphrey and Charles Weidman to run the Denishawn School in New York City.

In 1927, Doris Humphrey and Charles Weidman gave their first independent concert in New York City, for which they received great critical acclaim. When Shawn and St. Denis returned to New York, Humphrey and Weidman announced that they were leaving the Denishawn School. The Humphrey-Weidman collaboration produced additional new ideas in the technique of modern dance. This company toured widely and choreographed many "classical" modern dances. Their students included such modern dancers as Jose Limon, Sybil Shearer, Anna Halprin, Bill Bales, and Pauline Koner. The Humphrey-Weidman studio closed in 1945 when Doris Humphrey was forced to retire because of crippling arthritis (McDonagh, 1976). The Humphrey-Weidman Company was also not invited to perform at Jacob's Pillow, although Charles Weidman and Company danced there in 1947 and 1954.

In 1926, Martha Graham gave her first independent dance recital, with Louis Horst as her accompanist. He had traveled extensively overseas and had spent time in Germany and Austria. He had learned about the revolutionary German expressionist dancer, Mary Wigman. Horst was intrigued by Wigman's minimalist approach to music, as she employed only flutes, gong, drums, and occasionally, a piano.

> The prime purpose [of music] was to provide a background atmosphere that would enhance the dramatic or lyrical qualities of her dances. First and foremost for Wigman were her inwardly alive images and those spontaneous impulses that sparked her creativity....Yet...her approach brought up other problems—problems of dance composition....Clearly, dance composition was a craft that had to be mastered. (Stodelle, 1984, pp.41-42)

Louis Horst began to teach dance composition to Graham's students in 1928, and his book, *Pre-Classic Dance Forms* (1937), became a text for the generations that followed. Research Participant #VII recalled that she had studied composition with Horst.

In his biography of Martha Graham, Don McDonagh discussed the several influences upon Graham during her post-Denishawn period. He cited "Central European Expressionist dance as Graham understood it from books and pictures that Horst had brought back from Germany" (McDonagh, 1973, p.54). He described Martha Graham and her pupils studying Wigman's pictures as they tried to understand this new form of choreography that was attempting "to speak directly and forcefully to the time, to its disillusionment and privation. This was exactly what Graham wanted to do in her art" (McDonagh, 1973, p.54).

Graham's contributions to emerging field of American modern dance were many: she was an innovative and prolific choreographer, and she presented a new vision of what dance could become. Her most important contribution was the development of an original technique or style of movement. Agnes deMille, a dancer and choreographer of renown, discussed Graham's technique in her biography of Martha Graham.

Martha stripped off the chassis of the body and exposed the motor. She got the gestures down to not only the muscles, which is 'how,' but to the juices and the electricity as well, which is 'why'....She concentrated on the torso as the source of life, the motor....

The spasm of the diaphragm, the muscles used in coughing and laughing, were used to spark gesture. There was a shutting and downward movement, and an opening and lifting of both the diaphragm and the pelvis. These spasms she called contractions. And they were visible...not just in the resulting effect but in what they caused the rest of the body to do....

In the Graham technique, the arms and legs moved as a result of

this spasm of percussive force....the force of the movement passes from
the pelvis and diaphragm to the extremities, neck and head. (deMille,
1991, pp.96-98)

We can observe the evolutionary process of modern dance evolving as we
review these first two generations of dancers. Martha Graham was a student of
Ted Shawn and Ruth St. Denis, and she studied the photographs of Mary
Wigman. Graham actually met Wigman several times. In 1930, Sol Hurok
brought Wigman to America for the first time. Martha Graham, Doris Humphrey,
and Charles Weidman attended her performance and the welcoming party.
However, competition among the modern dancers at that moment in time was so
intense that the American dancers were unenthusiastic.

They were even less happy when Sol Hurok insisted upon the opening of
the Mary Wigman School in New York City, threatening to withdraw his support
of the Company if Wigman did not open a school. However, Wigman chose to
return to Germany, and sent her pupil Hanya Holm to run the new school. This
school ultimately served to expand the public's awareness of modern dance
(McDonagh, 1973, pp.86-87).

In 1954, Martha Graham and her company toured Europe and received
great acclaim. However, when the company reached Berlin, "Mary Wigman was
exuberant and emotional...throwing herself on the ground and kissing Martha's
feet. Her demonstration was homage indeed, coming from the high priestess and
leader of the entire European modern movement" (deMille, 1991, p.316).

The interweaving of the careers of these first two generations of modern
dancers is important because it illustrates the evolutionary continuum in a
concrete manner.

The field of psychology also evolved in such a way that one generation
greatly influenced the next, either in a positive or negative manner. All of Martha
Graham's biographers document her connection to Carl Jung, the great Swiss
psychoanalyst, who was an early disciple of Sigmund Freud. Jung was one of the

earliest dissidents from the Freudian point of view: he developed his own school of thought and training institutes throughout the world.

Dr. Frances Wickes was trained by Jung, and was Graham's psychotherapist for many years. "If Martha was not formally a patient of Frances Wickes, she was dependent on her, seeing her at least once a week when they were in the same city. When Martha was away, she wrote and wrote" (deMille, 1991, p.308).

Graham actually met Carl Jung during her 1954 European tour. Dr. Wickes had arranged for Jung and his wife to entertain Graham when she visited Switzerland, and they also attended her concert (deMille, 1991, p.316).

However, Graham's connection to Jung was more professionally relevant than her relationship to Wickes. In 1935, Martha Graham started to teach at Sarah Lawrence College, in Bronxville, New York. She met Joseph Campbell there, who taught mythology, anthropology, and classical history at the College. Jean Erdman was a dance student at Sarah Lawrence and became a member of Graham's company. She subsequently married Joseph Campbell.

In 1949, Graham participated in the Bennington School of the Arts along with the Campbells. According to deMille, Graham discussed the new dance she was working on, *Deaths and Entrances,* with Erdman and Campbell. Joseph Campbell introduced Graham to Jung's concept of the collective unconscious, and the significance of the myth. Graham was known for being an avid reader throughout her life and at that time, was currently studying eastern philosophies and symbolism. After her introduction by Campbell, Graham began to read the work of Jung.

The Jungian theories, together with the deeply spiritual concept of the kundalini, which had been worked through to a manifest and practical system, seemed to bring enlightenment to Martha. It gave her a handle for her aesthetic manipulation....Movement in space...now became, with her new understanding, purposeful and revelatory. The finished dance…clearly took place in a greater scheme. (deMille, 1991, p.250)

Jung's ideas continued to inform the work of Martha Graham throughout the remainder of her career. Her continued discussions with Joseph Campbell supported her explorations, and her understanding of mythology. Agnes deMille interviewed Campbell extensively and has documented his views about Martha Graham:

> The more you know of myth or of psychology, the more you perceive. I have told many creative artists about my beliefs very often. They are intrigued but very few can translate this theoretical material into art. Martha is truly the only one who can transform the material into a masterpiece with her perception. Here psychological linkings are worked through her own experiences to emerge fresh and living. (deMille, 1991, p.278)

Graham used her enriched perceptions in the choreography of the dances known as the Greek pieces. These dances include *Herodiade, Cave of the Heart, Clytemnestra, Errand into the Maze, Alcestis, Phaedra, Circe, Andromache's Lament,* and *Phaedra's Dream* (deMille, 1991, pp.434-455).

In 1937, Martha Graham wrote an essay discussing modern dance and the reasons for its development. This essay is significant for many reasons: deMille documented Graham's desire to leave behind a legacy, rather than a biography, and described how Graham had systematically destroyed all of her personal documents (such as letters to her mother, her sisters, and her lovers). *The Notebooks of Martha Graham,* (1973), includes many ideas for her dances—those completed, and those never finished—and many references to her extensive reading. However, very little of Graham's actual writing is available to the researcher.

In the 1937 essay, Graham wrote that the essential function of dance was to communicate. She noted the transitions that had occurred from 18th century thinking, and reflected that there were different sources of inspiration for the dance in the 20th century.

> Once we strove to imitate gods....Then we strove to become part of nature. [Therefore] dance was no longer performing its function of communication.
>
> This is the reason for the appearance of the modern dance....The old forms could not give voice to the more fully awakened man. (Graham, 1937, pp.50-51)

Graham (1937) stated that modern dance developed after World War I because this period demanded "new forms for the reborn man to inhabit" (p. 51). It was therefore necessary that new forms and new techniques be developed for the basic instrument, the human body.

Graham (1937) also noted that this revolt had occurred in response to the "ornamented, forms of impressionistic dancing" (p.51). She was alluding to the choreography of Isadora Duncan and her first two teachers, Ted Shawn and Ruth St. Denis.

Graham spoke about the new type of dance in which movement was used carefully and with significance so that the subject matter of the dance could be observed. She reflected upon the need for the development of a dynamic technique that could be performed with costuming stripped to the barest essentials. Graham (1937) also discussed the new manner in which music was being used, as music would no longer be the emotional stimulus of the dance, but the background of the dance, stating, "As dance evolved into the larger forms, music began to evolve also. The composer gained a greater strength and a more significant line from composing to meeting the requirements of the dance" (p.52). Martha Graham was one of the first American choreographers who collaborated with modern composers, just as Mary Wigman had done in the previous generation.

The final subject discussed by Graham (1937) in this essay was stage décor. She reflected that one must consider a spatial orientation on the stage, and the manner in which this connects to the choreography and the scenery. She advocated for a new spatial awareness, and a décor that could be employed to enhance both movement and gesture (pp.50-53).

Martha Graham's 1937 essay provides an enlightening view of an exceptional artist reflecting upon the impact of the zeitgeist upon her work. Her viewpoint owed more to the ideas of Mary Wigman than to Ted Shawn and Ruth St. Denis.

Hanya Holm. Hanya Holm is the fifth of the modern dancers who will be discussed in this study. Although born in Germany, Holm had a powerful impact upon the evolution of American modern dance. Hanya Holm was born in 1893 in Worms-am-Rein; she died in 1992. She attended the Conservatory of Music in Frankfurt and then spent four years at the Dalcroze Institute. In 1921, Holm saw Mary Wigman dance, and elected to join her group.

When Holm recalled those early days with Wigman, she said:

> She was like an ocean that always came back to you, and always renewed. Whatever new vision came to her required a new discovery, and the idea was, how shall one go about expressing this idea best? The wonderful thing in those days was that there was no preconceived method in existence, no preconceived patterns, the pattern changing with the demand, and with the invention of expressing the new idea. (Sorrell, 1969, p.18)

Holm thus reflected the innovative era in German Expressionistic Dance, when each and every movement was subject to examination. Nothing was to be taken for granted. Improvisation was a mandated method of exploration. It is important to understand the improvisational origins of Holm's teaching and choreography. Many of the third generation of modern dancers referred to Holm's improvisational methods in their interviews, believing that they had benefited tremendously from this approach. One of Holm's students, Alwin Nikolais, became a master of new styles and forms, sharing this knowledge with two dancers of the third generation who were interviewed in this study.

Hanya Holm (1951), in her article, "The Mary Wigman I know," added important historical and psychological perspectives to the German Expressionistic dance movement. In this 1951 essay, Holm recalled the post-World War I Germans, conquered and defeated, seeking to find new values to sustain them during this period of uncertainty. Holm thought "the individual discovered himself in relation to his fellow-man and the universe. Mary Wigman gave it artistic expression through movement" (Holm, 1951, p.25).

In this essay, Holm compared Wigman to Isadora Duncan, recalling Duncan's emphasis upon the divine expression of the human spirit through bodily movement.

> What was still lyrical romanticism in…Duncan became in…Wigman the dramatic interpretation of the conflicts within the individual and in relation to the influence of the outside world.
>
> When man is the eternal and unchanging theme of the dance, then…these themes are constantly changing with man's conditions and his fate.…Man must find his own language of expression in every epoch. (1951, p.25)

During the 1920s, the Wigman School offered a haven for another group of innovators, a group of musicians. The young men who accompanied Wigman's classes exemplified the revolution that was occurring in German music. The accompanists included " Hindemith, and Schöenberg, Satie, Krenek, and Bartok, and they pushed the classics from the studios and dances of the Wigman students" (Sorell, 1969, p.26).

This connection between the revolutionary dancer/choreographers and the newest forms of music developed under the auspices of the Wigman schools. The other members of the first generation of modern dancers, Ruth St. Denis, Ted Shawn, and even Isadora Duncan, selected classical forms of music for their teaching and their choreography. Martha Graham and Hanya Holm followed the Wigman example of teaching and choreographing to the most modern forms of music. The third generation of modern dancers experimented with all forms of music, daring to choreograph to commissioned music (Participant #9), to popular music (Participant #10), or to use no music at all (Participant #7).

Holm discussed another important aspect of German contemporary culture during that post World War I era: psychology. Holm once again compared the environments in which Isadora Duncan and Mary Wigman had lived and worked.

> When Isadora began to dance at the turn of the century, modern psychology was in its incipient stages. When Mary Wigman toured Germany for the first time in the bitter winter of 1919-20, modern psychology had come of age.
>
> What was with Isadora Duncan "soul and beauty" became with Mary Wigman the transparency of the individual's psychological manifestations—in the Jungian rather than the Freudian sense—with the subtleties of all emotional shadings. (Holm, 1951, p.25)

This remarkable paragraph illuminates many aspects of this researcher's inquiry. One might imagine that the literate dancer/choreographers were familiar with the psychologists of the era in which they lived. Martha Graham was well versed in the writings and ideas of Carl Jung. However, there is amazingly little documentation of this type of knowledge in the autobiographies and biographies of Ted Shawn, Ruth St. Denis, and Mary Wigman.

Wigman is the most puzzling, since we have read about her summers spent in the revolutionary environment of Ascona, beginning in 1913. The work of Sigmund Freud had already been carried to the United States in 1909, when he traveled to Clark University with his colleagues, Carl Jung and Sandor Ferenczi. Jung had broken with Freud in 1912, and was becoming increasingly well known in Europe (Grosskurth, 1991, pp.36-52).

However, Wigman did not discuss psychology in either of her books. In *The Mary Wigman Book,* 1973, there are numerous highly personal letters to Dr. Herbert Binswanger, who was described only as a "very close friend" (Sorrell, 1973, p.289).

Hanya Holm was the only dancer/choreographer who reflected a comprehension of the role that the writings of Sigmund Freud and Carl Jung might have played in the evolving German Expressionist Dance Movement. Holm described the work of Mary Wigman, alluding to the Jungian concept of the collective unconscious.

> Her creations are unsophisticated. She draws from rich sources of symbolic-primitive origin....Her intellect works as a moderating, controlling factor. It elevates her topics to a level of universal importance.
>
> In her *Witches Dance,* (1926)...it was not her idea of visualizing broomstick or Walpurgis Night, but the deepbedded darkness in man, the wicked and witch-like trends in the human character. (1951, p.20)

Hanya Holm studied with Mary Wigman for 10 years, developing into a teacher and choreographer at the school in Dresden. However, Holm elected to leave Germany. She arrived in New York City in 1931 to open the first Mary Wigman School in the United States. In 1932, Sol Hurok turned the Mary Wigman School over to Hanya Holm. In 1936, Holm debuted her own dance company (Cristofori, 1998, p.358).

In 1932, Holm returned to Germany to exchange her visitor's visa for an immigration visa because she had decided to become an American citizen. Holm was amazed by the attitudes of her American students and their outlook upon life.

Initially, she was taken aback by "Their points of view, by their philosophy of life. The feeling that nothing is impossible, that everything goes, the opportunistic attitude, and the one that you can buy what you want" (Sorell, 1969, p.37).

Holm was quick to realize that New York City was not America, and she began to travel throughout the United States. Hanya's name was becoming well known, and she had many opportunities to teach as she traveled. In 1932, Holm taught at Mills College in California, and she taught at the Perry-Mansfield Camp in Colorado in 1933. She was invited to become a faculty member at the Bennington School of the Dance from 1934 through 1941. In 1941, Hanya Holm established the renowned summer program at Colorado College, in Colorado Springs, where she continued to teach for the next 43 years (Cristofori, 1998, p.358).

In addition to running the Wigman school in New York City and teaching at the famous summer schools of dance, Holm took the opportunity to lecture on the differences between German and American modern dance. She spoke at The New School for Social Research, Columbia University, and many other schools. She also wrote an essay in which she juxtaposed the German and American approaches to the evolution of the modern dance field. Holm stressed the differences in the approaches to art, and the impatience and hastiness of the Americans, as compared to the patience of the Europeans who had the time to explore through trial and error (Holm, 1935).

In 1933, Hitler seized power in Germany. The anti-Nazi sentiment was very strong within the dance community in New York City, and people became suspicious of the Wigman School itself. After consultation with Mary Wigman, who had chosen to remain in Germany, Holm changed the name of the school to the Hanya Holm School of Dance. Holm found it necessary to issue a statement avowing complete tolerance and creative freedom and disavowing "any political creed which strangles the free development of art" (Sorell, 1969, p.45).

Once again, Holm reflected her understanding of how the world around her was changing, and she took definitive action. Wigman was the only other member of the first and second generations of modern dancer/choreographers to reflect upon, to discuss, and to take action in response to the major events of the 20th century. The other members of this group appear to have had few political ties and less involvement. The third generation of American modern dancers discussed politics, made political statements, and took action in response to contemporary politics.

As a teacher, Holm continued to develop new ideas and added innovative classes to her schools. She was the first dance teacher to have anatomy taught in her studio, and then she added training in percussion instruments. As a teacher, who was intimately familiar with the impact of the zeitgeist, Holm lectured her students about the connections between dance and other art forms.

> To give her students deeper insight into the past and its social function she would prove her wide frame of reference by citing examples of previous days; and...she had John Martin, then dance critic of *The New York Times*, teach dance history in her studios. (Sorell, 1969, p.47)

Holm was the first modern dancer to travel to many colleges, with her lecture-demonstrations. This, too, was an innovation, because Holm was thus bringing modern dance to the small schools throughout the United States. These tours took place during the 1930s, creating a new audience for the barefoot dancers who represented the new voices of modern dance. Even the form of the lecture-demonstration was a Holm creation that allowed her to show the audience exactly what she meant, while she explained it theoretically.

Hanya Holm was an innovative dance teacher, director of dance schools, and a lecturer in the evolving field of modern dance in the 1930s and 1940s. Her choreography was revolutionary as well, because she integrated her training with Mary Wigman into dances that were reflective of contemporary events.

Holm's masterwork, *Trend*, was first presented at Bennington College in 1937, and premiered at the New York City Center later that year. It was considered a monumental dance, with a cast of more than 30 dancers and with music by Wallingford Riegger and Edgar Varese. This dance

> ...offered a symbolic vision of world conditions from World War I to the 1930's....Scenes represented industrial regimentation, the self-indulgence of the leisured class, the desire for money, fanatical religion and political despotism....After this evocation of social disintegration, *Trend* concluded with images of resurgence and assurance. (Anderson, 1997, pp.147-148)

Once again, Holm was reflecting and commenting upon the zeitgeist of the world in which she was living and creating. Dances of this scope and subject matter were unique in the United States in the 1930s. *The Green Table*, by Kurt Jooss, was choreographed in Germany in 1931, and later became a "classic" repertory piece of the Robert Joffrey Ballet Company in the 1960s (Terry, 1956, p.155).

Another significant part of Holm's professional career was her development and administration of, the Summer Dance Program at Colorado College in Colorado Springs. She ran the program for 43 years, and taught many of the classes herself. The curriculum included such courses as dance technique, theory, composition, music for dance, Labanotation, and dance pedagogy. This program was 8 weeks long (Sorell, 1969, pp.90-91). Many of Holm's students became famous professional dancers, and were subsequently invited to teach at this summer school (three of the research participants in this study taught there).

Holm dissolved her dance company in 1944, which also ended her career as a dancer. In the next phase of her career, Holm began to choreograph for the Broadway theater. In 1948, Holm was invited to choreograph *The Eccentricities of Davey Crockett* and *Kiss Me Kate*. She found herself receiving outstanding reviews from the New York critics. Holm arranged for all of the dances from *Kiss Me Kate* to be notated by Ann Hutchinson (Labanotation teacher and expert), and in 1952, Holm registered the first complete choreographic score of dances to be copyrighted. This script, now printed on microfilm, is currently on file at the Library of Congress in Washington, DC (Sorell, 1969, pp.108-114).

Holm continued to choreograph for the musical stage, including such plays as *Out of This World* (1951), *My Darlin' Aida* (1952), *The Golden Apple* (1954), *My Fair Lady* (1956), the opera, *The Ballad of Baby Doe* (1956), *Where's Charley?* (1957), and *Camelot* (1960); (Cristofori, 1998, pp.356-357).

Holm taught at the Juilliard School, the Nikolais-Louis studio, and at the Colorado College Summer School until she was in her 90s. She never retired, which is typical of the dancers surveyed in this study. In 1985, she was celebrated as an "Honored Guest" at the American Film Institute at the Kennedy Center in Washington, DC. She repeated one of her most famous statements, which has been reprinted many times, and by which she will be long remembered, "You will find out that one life is not enough. You will want to have several lives in which to discover what there is to be discovered" (Cristofori, 1998, p.359).

Hanya Holm was a true revolutionary in the field of American modern dance, as a dancer, a choreographer, a teacher and as an innovative thinker. She was cited by four of the research participants in this study as their most influential teacher. Her talented pupil, Alvin Nikolais, trained two of the other dancers surveyed. Holm attained the stature of the four other leading dancers in this study, and she is remembered with deep love by her students and colleagues.

The Dance Therapists

Dance/movement therapy has been defined as "the psychotherapeutic use of movement as a process which furthers the emotional, social, cognitive, and physical integration of the individual" (American Dance Therapy Association, 2001). This literature review of dance/movement therapists was undertaken to explore the connections between these professionals and the founders of humanistic psychology. Many of the dance/movement therapists have written extensively about their profession, and their work is as diverse as they are.

Marian Chace. Any literature review of dance/movement therapists must begin with Marian Chace, the "mother" of dance therapy in the United States.

Chace was born in 1896 and died in 1970. Chace was trained by Ted Shawn, Ruth St. Denis, and Martha Graham. Chace was a member of the Denishawn dancers and toured with the company from 1927 to 1930. Chace opened a branch of the Denishawn School in Washington, DC in 1930 (Hoffman, 1999c).

Marian Chace evolved gradually into a dance therapist during the next 10 years, during which time she taught a variety of special populations who challenged her to develop new ideas. She wrote:

> I began to be aware of the needs these people were expressing through their bodies....I spent many hours in contemplation, and found the understanding of the communications.

> Instead of feeling frustrated with them when they lagged behind...I tried to empathize with them as people. Obviously, my teaching was undergoing change. (Chace, 1993, p.12)

Chace worked with children from clinics, orphanages, girls from the National Training School (a correctional facility), and individuals referred by pediatricians, psychologists, and psychiatrists (Hoffman, 1999c, p.10). Chace's first training as a therapist began when she started receiving feedback from Dr. Agnes Bruce Greig, who had founded a clinic for disturbed children. Greig sent her pupils to work with Chace and then reviewed their progress, offering Chace her first professional supervision (Hoffman, 1999c, pp.10-11).

In 1942, Marian Chace began to work at St. Elizabeth's Hospital in Washington, DC. This was a federal psychiatric hospital that was understaffed because of World War II, and overloaded with the wounded from many battlefields. Chace began to work in the psychodrama department, under the supervision of Dr. Roscoe Hall, Chief of psychotherapy, and Frances Herriot, a psychodramatist. Chace wrote:

Dr. Hall...was very much interested in music, painting and all of the arts as a means of communication for patients and...these people gave tremendous support to me as I began to work with tools and techniques never before attempted with the mentally ill in a hospital setting. (1975, p.19)

While Chace developed her ideas and techniques at St. Elizabeth's Hospital, she also received clinical training. She attended the daily case conferences at the hospital and took classes at the Washington School of Psychiatry, which was headed by Harry Stack Sullivan during the 1940s. She studied basic psychiatry, adjunctive therapies, art therapy, and assessment of the mentally ill, under Dr. Frieda Fromm-Reichmann (Hoffman, 1999c, p.16).

Fromm-Reichmann was to become an important teacher for Chace because of her interest in Chace's pioneering work. Fromm-Reichmann was herself a therapeutic pioneer and one of the neo-Freudian group of thinkers. She was associated with Chestnut Lodge, a small, private psychiatric hospital that specialized in the long-term care of psychotic patients. Marian Chace was invited to join Chestnut Lodge by Fromm-Reichmann, and worked there from 1946 to 1966.

Harry Stack Sullivan was another famous neo-Freudian who also had an impact upon the ideas of Marian Chace. He supervised the Chestnut Hill staff during the first two years that Chace worked there as a dance therapist (Hoffman, 1999c, p.20).

Marian Chace's connection to these two neo-Freudians is relevant to this study. The neo-Freudians as a group were responsible for changing the classical European form of psychiatry into a less rigid, more American, interpersonal form of psychotherapy. My earlier studies of the impact of the neo-Freudians upon the works of Abraham Maslow, Rollo May, Carl Rogers, and James Bugental, illustrated that the neo-Freudians served as the teachers and role models for many of the humanistic psychologists.

Chace's interactions with Fromm-Reichmann and Sullivan were essential to her ongoing clinical training, and were reflected in her later work (Hoffman, 1999c, pp.17, 21-23).

Chace's writings were simply phrased and expressed. It has been the work of the second and third generations of dance/movement therapists to interpret and elucidate what Chace meant. Chace never wrote that the theories of Fromm-Reichmann and Sullivan had any impact upon her work or upon her ideas. The connections between the writings of Marian Chace and her two great clinical teachers were made either by this researcher, or by the other dance therapists who have studied her writings.

For example, Fromm-Reichmann (1950), writing about schizophrenics, suggested that a "doctor's nonverbal concomitants of the psychotherapeutic exchange are equally, if not...more important than the verbal contents of communication" (p.202). She advocated that patients be taught to observe and describe their physical symptoms, and the times and places of occurrence. Finally, Fromm-Reichmann stated that "dance was one of the ways in which a patient might turn his or her symptomotology into a creative asset" (p.13).

When Chace wrote about the use of dance as an adjunctive therapy for hospitalized mental patients, she stated:

> In the psychotic, language loses much of its effectiveness as a means of relating to others....The seriously ill mental patient relies to a large extent on nonverbal devices for the communication of his emotions....Muscular activity expressing emotion is the substratum of dance, and since dance is a means of structuring and organizing such activity, dance could be a potent means of communication with and reintegration of the seriously ill mental patient. (Chace, 1975, p.71)

Fromm-Reichmann also stressed the identification of the healthiest aspects of the patient, in order to allow the therapist to work with these parts. This encouraged healthier overall functioning for the hospitalized patient.

Fran Levy (1988), in her book *Dance/Movement Therapy: A Healing Art*, clearly linked the work of Marian Chace to that of the humanistic psychologists. She stated that

> Humanistic theory's major contribution is in its emphasis on the uniqueness of individuals, and on methods of releasing humanity's creative and expressive potential....It seeks out the health and potential in the personality rather than pathology and weakness and in doing so opens the doors of expression to many different idioms, dance, drama, and music, art. (p.12)

Levy acknowledged that Chace had always sought and attempted to engaged those parts of the patient's personality that were seeking to be heard, and to be well. Levy (1988) stated, "In this respect, Chace was to the in-hospital patient in the 1940's what the humanistic psychologists Maslow (1968, 1978), and Rogers (1961) were to 'healthy' patients in the 1960s" (p.24).

Chace was also directly influenced by Sullivan's ideas about the role of the group leader. Sullivan advocated that the group leader should become a part of the healing process in the new role of participant observer, and therefore help to facilitate change and healing (Chapman, 1976). Chace (1964) used these ideas to describe the involvement of the dance therapist: "Direct communication must happen continuously between the group and the leader...[then] a strong and useful relationship will develop between the leader and the patient; and from there between the patient and others in the group" (p.47). The role of the dance therapist is clearly to be a facilitator, and to engage as a participant observer during any group session. Chace clearly understood the importance of the interactions between her hospitalized patients and the dance therapist. She employed Sullivan's concept of the participant observer, approaching the most regressed patients with a gesture or movement that resembled their own. She understood the need to reply in movement, making the dance into a shared, healing experience.

Marian Chace did not credit either Frieda Fromm-Reichmann or Harry Stack Sullivan for their ideas, that she integrated into her work. However,she was influenced by them both, making her a significant bridge between dance, dance therapy, and humanistic psychology.

Penny Bernstein Lewis. Penny Bernstein, a student of Marian Chace, graduated from Saybrook Graduate School, formerly the Humanistic Psychology Institute. Her edited book, *Eight Theoretical Approaches in Dance/movement Therapy* (Bernstein, 1979), was based upon her dissertation, which she wrote under the chairmanship of Rollo May.

Bernstein's book contained articles written by dance/movement therapists, who described how they had applied a variety of psychological theories to the field of dance/ movement therapy. There are articles written by therapists who utilized the work of C. G. Jung, Alfred Adler, Sigmund Freud, and F.C. Perls. Other chapters discuss Marian Chace's approach, Trudi Schoop's ideas about dance therapy, as well as the psychodynamic, and the transpersonal-transformational frameworks of therapy.

Dr. Lewis (formerly Penny Bernstein) stated, "The summary, of course, reflected a humanistic viewpoint. I'm certain you saw that" (Personal communication, February 28, 2000). Lewis was referring to her summary of the theories of dance/movement therapy, which appeared at the conclusion of her book.

Lewis maintains a unique position within the second generation of dance/movement therapists; she trained with Marian Chace (at the Turtle Bay Music School in New York City). As of 2004, she is an associate faculty member at the Antioch-New England Graduate School, and continues to teach and conduct a private practice.

Lewis acknowledged her wish to "ground dance/movement therapy in theoretical constructs" (personal communication, February 28, 2000). She has accomplished this, having published many articles, books, and articles that are focused upon illustrating and illuminating the theoretical structures of her profession. However Lewis (1993) stated reflectively,

> As I look back on nearly 25 years in this field and on those elements which have been the most important, many can be traced back to my training with Marian Chace....After all these years, I know just how important theory is and how unimportant it is as well. Marian worked from intuition. She employed the imaginal realm, meeting patients where they were, and bringing them into an experience of potential healing. (pp.154-155)

Lewis then took Chace's ideas, intuitively developed and simply expressed, and presented them within her own theoretical frameworks. The most intriguing aspect of this theoretical presentation is that it does not include any of the ideas of Maslow, May, Rogers, or Bugental.

Lewis has integrated object relations, ego psychology, and Jungian theory, and employed a developmental structure for her synthesized theoretical stance. However, she has completely neglected the humanistic psychologists, both the original founders and the more contemporary theoreticians.

Ilene Serlin. Ilene Serlin is a member of the third generation of dance/movement therapists, and has published many articles discussing the use of movement as a therapeutic modality. Serlin has frequently demonstrated the linkage between the ideas of the humanistic psychologists and the work of the dance/movement therapist.

The words of Carl Rogers and James Bugental resonate clearly through her 1989 article, "Movement Composition and the Choreography of a Verbal Psychotherapy Session," which appeared in *The Psychoaesthetic Experience* (1989).

Serlin (1989) discussed how she demonstrated her ability to be completely present during the session, so as to assist her client to evolve and transform. She stated, "Through my active setting of boundaries and use of presence, she [the client] was able to experience a moment of congruence between inner and outer self, and we were able to experience an integrated relationship together" (p.56).

This ability to be fully present within the therapeutic relationship has been discussed at length by Bugental (1987) in *The Art of The Psychotherapist*. According to Bugental, "Presence is...a quality of being in a situation or a relationship in which one intends at a deep level to participate...fully" (p.27). Such a quality in the therapist creates a level of attention and caring, which then produces a new level of response from the client. Serlin demonstrated this concept in her work with her clients.

Another important aspect of Serlin's work was her strongly empathic connection with her clients. Serlin did not merely see what was happening in the session, she sensed and she felt her client's needs, and she moved swiftly (and physically). Serlin (1989) describes how she held her client's body in its tumultuous state, so as to contain, re-parent, and assist with the reintegrative process of therapy (p.56).

Carl Rogers has written at great length about the empathic connection that is so desirable when working with another person. Rogers (1975) discussed several aspect of empathy, such as, "The ability to enter an other's private world, to be able to sense the flow of changing feelings, and becoming a confident companion to the other person within this world" (p.5). Rogers' ideas are strongly reflected in the article by Serlin.

In her article, "Therapy with a Borderline Nun," Serlin (1990) employed Rollo May's ideas about the creative process to guide the therapeutic direction of her work. Serlin stated, "A successful artist is one who can be submerged in the unconscious or chaos, and find form in it" (p.93). Working with this client, Serlin was able to reframe the issues confronting her. In collaboration with the nun, Serlin was able to understand the therapeutic problem as a breakdown of form, or the absence of a center that could give shape to her life. The therapeutic goals could then be formulated as the need to recreate structure in the nun's life, and ultimately to create her own personal "holding environment." These goals were concrete, but the results were expansive.

When Serlin (1990) summarized the treatment, she stated, "For [the nun] and me, dancing together was a language and a process to heal her splits between psychology and religion, mind and body, God and evil. Art was our language, as our therapy was form of healing art" (p.93).

Rollo May's ideas about the healing qualities of the artistic process were explored in depth in *The Courage to Create*) (1975). Once again, Serlin has employed the ideas and concepts of one of the pioneers of humanistic psychology, and found them applicable to and illuminating for her work as a therapist.

Chapter 3

Research Methodology

This research study employed a qualitative research methodology, using a systematic thematic analysis to discover the "lived experiences and meanings" (Luborsky, 1994, p.190). To collect this data, I interviewed a group of the pioneers of American modern dance.

The portion of my research proposal, which was accepted by the Saybrook Institutional Review Board on September 17, 2000, was to interview a group of modern dancers. The requirements for the research subjects were specific: each dancer/choreographer must have had a concrete connection to the Jacob's Pillow Dance Festival, i.e., either as a student, a performer, or a teacher. In addition, each potential interviewee had to be linked to one of the major choreographic families as listed by Don McDonagh (1976). My goal was to interview one representative of at least four of the following "families:" Martha Graham, Merce Cunningham, Paul Taylor, Doris Humphrey, and Charles Weidman; Anna Sokolow, José Limón, Hanya Holm, Helen Tamiris, and Lester Horton. A consultation and collaboration with Norton Owen, Director of Preservation at Jacob's Pillow, produced a list of potential research participants.

Data Collection Procedures

Participant recruiting. On September 25, 2000, I mailed a total of 19 letters to the following dancer/choreographers: Mary Anthony, Robby Barnett,

Carolyn Brown, Trisha Brown, Merce Cunningham, Carmen deLavallade, Lester Horton, Bill T. Jones, Phyllis Lamhut, Murray Louis, Pauline Koner, Jim May, Carla Maxwell, Daniel Nagrin, Don Redlich, Jennifer Scanlon, Paul Taylor, Glenn Tetley, and Twyla Tharp. See Appendix A for a copy of this letter.

Informed consent. Each letter contained an Informed Consent Form (Appendix B), along with a stamped, self-addressed envelope. Eight of the letters included a handwritten note at the bottom of the page, requesting that the Informed Consent Form be returned as soon as possible so that an interview could be scheduled promptly. The question in this researcher's mind (which prompted the handwritten note) was, would this note facilitate a more rapid response from the potential interviewee? The answer proved to be a definitive no: only two of the potential research participants returned the form and their letters lacked the handwritten note. In fact, the Informed Consent Form proved to be the stumbling block for most of the participants. They were initially reluctant to sign it because they were uncertain about its meaning; and they asked for explanations of its contents. Several of them misplaced the form several times, even after the form was explained at length in the follow-up phone calls.

Interview Scheduling. Three of the dancers returned the form quickly, and one interview was held on October 1, 2000. I scheduled the next two interviews after October 15, 2000. The follow-up phone calls were made three weeks after the letters were sent out, and I was able to schedule two interviews during the second week in November. An interview was held on November 17, 2000, and another on December 1, and another on December 16. At the same time, I received letters and phone calls from two other potential interviewees, who told me about their travels and offered to speak with me in late December or early January. The final two interviews were scheduled on January 9, 2001, and January 11, 2001.

One interview was actually held twice due to faulty recording equipment. When I questioned the dissertation chair about the "lost interview" and how it should be handled within the numerical sequence of the interviews, he suggested that I request another interview. The participant most graciously agreed to be interviewed for a second time, and whatever could be salvaged from the original interview was combined with the content of the second interview. The 10 complete interviews comprise the data considered in the analysis.

Interviews: Protocol and Conduct.

The interview protocol was a semi-structured interview (Appendix C) that covered three primary topics. The first area of interest was the participant's dance background: when did they begin to study dance, who were their teachers, what types of dance did they study, who did they consider were their most important teachers, and why were these particular teachers so important to them?

The second topic of interest to the researcher was The Jacob's Pillow Dance Festival and each participant's experiences there. The questions in this section of the protocol dealt with the impact of "The Pillow" upon the participant, whether as a student, a teacher, or a performer. The interview included questions about the people they met at The Pillow, the actual physical site, their knowledge of the history of Jacob's Pillow, and how these factors might have affected their work as dancers/choreographers.

The final series of questions focused upon psychology, the participants' knowledge of the literature, and any experiences they might have had with psychotherapy. They were asked specifically about their knowledge of Rollo May, Abraham Maslow, Carl Rogers, and James Bugental. Additionally, I asked all participants whether they had made any personal connections between their readings in psychology, personal psychotherapeutic experiences, if any, and the development of their professional work. Appendix C contains the interview protocol.

Data Processing and Storage. Each interview was then duplicated, numbered, dated, and submitted to a professional transcriber, who transcribed verbatim. Only the number of the interview and the date were used for identification. The typist was instructed to do a true verbatim transcription, i.e., to type only what she had heard, to add nothing, and to leave sentences incomplete if that is what she heard.

When the interview transcriptions were returned, I compared them with the audiotape and made corrections. These corrections were added to the floppy disk (provided by the transcriber), and two copies of each interview were printed on color-coded paper. One copy of each interview, with one copy of the cassette recording, and the floppy disk, were stored in a locked metal file in my office. Another copy of the interview and the original cassette were stored in a locked metal file at my home. In addition, each corrected interview was stored in my home computer and on a Zip disk at home. Therefore, there were always a total of seven copies of each interview available.

Conducting the Interviews

I gave each of the research participants a choice of the time and place for the interview: he or she could be interviewed by telephone, in my office in Manhattan or in his or her studio, or at home. One participant came to my office, 2 participants invited me to interview them at their studios, one at home, and the other 6 participants were interviewed by telephone. Of the 6 telephone interviewees, 4 of them were out of state (Connecticut, Massachusetts, Arizona, and New Mexico). The final 2 interviewees were so tightly scheduled that they felt they could only speak with me by telephone. I sent a personal thank you note was to each of the participants immediately after the interview.

My tape recording equipment proved to be excellent on the telephone and erratic for the in-person interviews. The interview in my office was lost almost completely and then rerecorded by telephone. A second live interview had huge gaps in the tape, which required extensive reconstruction on my part. This reconstruction was done immediately after the actual interview, and the notes were integrated into the transcription. I purchased second tape recorder for the in-person interviews.

"Interviewees in qualitative interviews share in the work of the interview, sometimes guiding it in a channel of their own choosing" (Rubin & Rubin, 1995, p.10). Many of the research participants were quite active in guiding the interviews, adding their own ideas and shaping the actual course of the interview. For example, Participant #1 brought the theme of religion into the interview repeatedly, illustrating its importance in her life and in her professional career. Participant #3 focused upon his own creative process, and the actual co-creating that occurs within his particular dance group. Participant #4 felt that his teaching experiences had formed an integral part of his career, which required an exploration during our interview.

Other research participants appeared to be very interested in me personally, in who I was, what I was doing, and why I was doing it. They asked questions that had already been answered in the original letter, and the Informed Consent Form and they asked many personal questions as well. I sought to be friendly but not self-revealing. My perusal of the literature of the qualitative research literature offered some guidance in this matter: "In qualitative interviewing, the researcher is not neutral, distant, or emotionally uninvolved....The researcher's empathy, sensitivity, humor, and sincerity are important tools for the research" (Rubin & Rubin, 1995, p.12).

My knowledge of the history of dance and my recall of many of the dancers' performances proved to be an asset and the interviewees responded to me very positively. When I had not actually seen the research participants in performance, I had done enough preliminary research to know what they had performed and when they had danced. Several of the dancer/choreographers expressed gratitude for my supportive questions and my empathic acknowledgement of their economic struggles.

Coding criteria. Arne Collen's Saybrook course in Qualitative Research Methods introduced various methods and techniques for coding interviews. I designed the interview protocol to explore three primary categories: the participant's dance training and teachers; recollections of the Jacob's Pillow experience, including the people, the history, and the actual site of this dance festival; knowledge of the four pioneers of humanistic psychology, the broader literature of psychology, and any psychotherapeutic experiences. This protocol was the basis for the coding for the themes found in the interviews.

> The qualitative research literature provides great support and encouragement for the coding by themes in interviews. First, thematic analysis is cited as a "direct representation of an individual's point of view and description of experiences, beliefs and perceptions....It exemplifies the goal of qualitative research, which aims to discover lived experiences and meanings. (Luborsky, 1994, p.190)

This is an exact description of what this portion of my research sought to explore. Many of the dancer/choreographers have written books, all of them have been previously interviewed, and their works have been reviewed. My hope was to allow them to speak in their own words on the three subjects I was researching.

Data Analysis

Luborsky assures us that "themes can be readily described and coded. It is relatively easy to reduce a lengthy stretch of talk to a phrase or label that describes the main point or theme of the passage" (1994, p.203). He also recommends the use of a worksheet on which to transcribe the themes as they appear within the interview (p. 203).

The utilization of a worksheet proved to be an invaluable asset to my coding. I developed a worksheet for each interview, on which I could color-code the topics and note the page numbers where each one occurred. This enabled me to observe repetitive phenomena and thematic material. It also became apparent that each interview had its own set of themes and variations that extended beyond the questions in the research protocol. The matrices for each interview illustrate this additional material.

> Data driven codes are constructed inductively from the raw information. They appear with the words and syntax of the raw information....The closeness of the code to raw information increases the likelihood that

various people examining the raw information will perceive and therefore encode the information similarly....Working directly from the raw information enhances appreciation of the information....With a complete view of the information available, the researcher can appreciate gross (i.e., easily evident) and intricate (i.e., difficult to discern) aspects of the information. (Boyatzis, 1998, p.30)

On the other hand, working directly from the raw information, as Boyatzis suggests, was also problematic for this researcher. The raw information was in actual transcriptions of the interviews. These transcriptions were 20 to 35 pages each in length. Luborsky, Boyatzis, and the Rubins all state that the qualitative researcher must review the raw material (in this case, the transcribed interviews) many times, so as to grasp the essence. "In code development...you may have to review each person's material 8 to 10 times" (Boyatzis, 1998, p.43).

I found that it was worthwhile to read each interview many times. Whatever themes emerged for coding on the first and second readings were supplemented on subsequent readings. "Coding proceeds in steps. First, you set up a few main coding categories, suggested by the original reading of the interviews" (Rubin & Rubin, 1995, p.239).

It was the subsequent reading and rereading of each interview that allowed the other ideas to emerge upon the worksheets. "Coding encourages hearing meaning in the data" (Rubin & Rubin, 1995, p.240). I used color-coded pens to present the visual cues clearly. I employed 50 separate colors in one interview. The use of so many colors required one additional step: the worksheets and the interview were color coded at the same time, rather than doing the interview first and worksheet at a later time.

It became clear through this process of rereading and color coding, that one can "code for themes, concepts and ideas, but you can also code for...stages or steps in a process" (Rubin & Rubin, 1995, p.241).

The developmental stages or steps within a dancer/choreographer's history are significant to an understanding of the person and the world in which their life is lived. Many of the participants were quite articulate about the evolution of their careers. They could pinpoint significant times and places and could discuss their own personal growth and evolution as dancers and as choreographers. They all could reflect upon the times they spent at Jacob's Pillow and whether or not it had an impact upon their lives in modern dance.

After I completed each worksheet, the coding was reviewed. The raw data were then grouped in larger categories: "Coding is the process of grouping interviewees' responses into categories that bring together the similar ideas, concepts or themes...discovered" (Rubin & Rubin, 1995, p.228).

These larger categories were also color-coded and became a synopsis of each interview. The synopses provided an illustration of what each interview had contained, and I converted this material into a matrix. "In the final stages of an analysis, the researcher organizes the data in ways that help formulate themes, refine concepts, and link them together to create a clear description or explanation of a culture or a topic" (Rubin & Rubin, 1995, p.251).

An individual summary of each research interview is presented in the order in which the interviews were actually conducted; i.e., Interview #1 took place on October 1, 2000, and Interview #10 was conducted on January 11, 2001. A final summary of all of the interviews is presented at the conclusion of the section on the research about the pioneers of modern dance. A case-ordered meta-matrix (Miles & Huberman, 1994) of the interview results for all of the participants is presented at the conclusion of the summary. A copy of this summary was sent to each of the research participants, with an additional note thanking them for participating in this study.

Chapter 4

Findings

Interview Content

This section presents the content of the interviews. This material was derived by the use of coding and analysis, techniques discussed in Chapter 3, Methodology. The discoveries made in that process are presented below in summary form for each of the 10 interviews; this is followed by a summary of the findings across all of the interviews.

Interview #1—October 1, 2000. The research participant for interview #1 was 85 years old in 2001. She is one of the two oldest members of this study. She remains professionally active in many ways. She returned to Jacob's Pillow on July 12-15, 2001, as a performer in *From the Horse's Mouth.* This is an improvisational piece of dance in which participants are asked to introduce themselves and then to select three cards that determine the individual's improvisation. Participant #1 introduced herself and apologized about her ability to dance, citing her age. She received an ovation at that time, and again later, when during the finale, clothed in a robe of many colors, she danced with other members of the cast.

She currently maintains a modern dance studio in Greenwich Village, where she teaches classes daily. A recent article in *The New York Times* described her teaching a class: "She accompanies the class on a large drum and suggests imagery: 'Imagine you're wearing big red boots. Now add four Chagall poses at the end. You all know Chagall's paintings?'" (Solomons, Jr., 2001). The utilization of imagery to convey meaning in dance is a recurrent theme in this interview. In addition to teaching, this participant continues to train her dance company. A review of her company's performances in December 2000 stated

> This company is something of a fixture in New York, and, at 44, is one of America's oldest companies. Yet it remains a vital creative instrument…it is one of the few companies that continues to perform the dance-theater repertoire of the 1950's and 1960's and do it well. (Garafola, 2001, p.84)

This interview was conducted in the participant's home, which is also the front room of her studio.

This participant was the only one who displayed a significant personal and professional connection to a religion, Roman Catholicism. Therefore, the theme of religion became an integral part of this interview. For example, she remembered "the beautifully costumed priests of my childhood, [their] backs to us" [Participant #1, p.3] as she recalled the beauty of the religious rituals she had seen since her childhood. She then made the connection between her religious life and her professional career, stating succinctly "Dancing is like going to church, you must do it regularly" [Participant #1, p.11].

These connections were explored throughout her career in modern dance, both in her dancing and in her choreography.

> In the 1950's she was one of the pioneers who brought serious modern dance to television, choreographing The Lord's Prayer for *Look Up and Live*, a Sunday morning religious show.…She choreographed 20 telecasts of *Look Up and Live*, and *Lamp unto My Feet* between 1957 and 1959. (Timm, 1996, pp.60-61)

This participant made other important connections as she combined her religious interests and her choreography. She participated with Ted Shawn and Ruth St. Denis in their Sacred Dance Guild during the years 1959, 1960, and 1961 (Shawn, 1960, p.283). During the 4th Annual Institute of the Sacred Dance Guild, which took place on at Jacob's Pillow on June 25-28, 1959, this participant was a featured teacher with Ted Shawn (Program, Jacob's Pillow Archives, inside page).

The Jacob's Pillow Dance festival represents another important theme in this interview. I thought that this participant's connection to Jacob's Pillow had been significant to her on many levels. She reflected upon the beauty of the actual physical site and how she had loved walking in the woods at The Pillow. She also acknowledged the historical impact of The Pillow and how Ted Shawn and his company, the Men Dancers, had actually constructed the original structure.

The research participant spoke fondly of Ted Shawn, recalling that "Ted had an Ego, you know, that big," [Participant #1, p. 7]. She stated her belief that the contributions of Ted Shawn and Ruth St. Denis had been underestimated, recalling that Martha Graham's original training came from the Denishawn School. Her personal fondness for The Pillow was stated clearly:

My whole memory of The Pillow is as a very warm, beautiful place. It was wonderful to be performing *Threnody* for a whole week. And Ted sent us flowers every night. He told me he did that because he always felt bad that Miss Ruth got flowers every night and he didn't. [Participant #1, p.9]

This interview subject also identified Ted Shawn's importance in other arenas, both historical and personal. She stated that she had great respect for what Ted had done for male dancers because he toured through the United States with his Men Dancers. This represented a major change in the position of men dancers, particularly in the 1930s. On a more personal level, she mentioned that she had seen this group: "I saw Ted Shawn and the Men Dancers when I was in school.

And I came home and said 'I'm going to marry Barton Mumaw'" [Participant #1, p.19]. (Barton Mumaw was one of the original group of men dancers in the 1930s, and he continued to perform for the next 50 years. He was also Ted Shawn's lover for many years (Sherman & Mumaw, 2000).

Another important theme that emerged from this interview was the impact of various dance teachers upon the interviewee. Her first modern dance teacher was a woman who had seen Mary Wigman perform; this teacher took her students to see Martha Graham in performance at a nearby university. The participant was motivated by this performance to come to New York City to continue her dance studies. She applied to the Graham studio for a scholarship, but because scholarships were not available, she studied with Hanya Holm. (Hanya Holm had been Mary Wigman's most famous student in Germany and had brought the Wigman technique to the United States.) The research participant acknowledged Holm as a teacher because "she allowed me to be me" [Participant #1, p.1]. However, Holm was mentioned only 4 times during the interview and Martha Graham is cited 10 times.

> I went to see the Graham studio and enrolled in the elementary class....I was put into the advanced class when Martha was still teaching every day, so I studied with her. So that was a very, very strong influence, not so much movement -wise, but in the way she'd get what she wanted out of the dancers. She gave us images....to get what she wanted into the movement. She would give you images of all kinds. [Participant #1, p.2]

This research participant identified many other influences upon her creativity, citing Greek theater, classical music, poetry, the Metropolitan Museum of Art, the Museum of Modern Art, and her many (22) summers at Fire Island.

Another theme that emerged from this interview was the influence of psychology upon the research participant. She reported that she had read Sigmund Freud, Carl Jung, and Wilhelm Reich. She believed that Reich had influenced her and her teaching with his ideas about character, and how much the body reveals. She had also read Karen Horney and Erich Fromm. She felt that the works of Horney and Fromm had nourished her and that their ideas had somehow influenced her choreography, although she could not specify how this had occurred.

She often reiterated the importance of images and how she used them in her teaching and in her choreography. The participant reflected that perhaps Jung's use of images had influenced her work and then said: "He very much influenced Martha, that I have read" [Participant #1, p.4]. The use of imagery, both in teaching and in choreography, is psychological device employed by many modern dancers. It differentiates certain schools of modern dance from the mechanistic or purely technical aspects of dance.

However, the participant was not familiar with the names of Abraham Maslow, Rollo May, Carl Rogers, and James Bugental. She stated that when it came to that group of psychologists, "I really should do some reading, yes? I'm out of touch, really out of touch" [Participant #1, p.18].

The most significant themes that emerged during this first interview were the participant's strong religious background, Ted Shawn and the Jacob's Pillow Dance Festival, Martha Graham and the various creative arts with which the participant surrounds herself. She employs these creative arts to enrich the images she uses to evoke texture and richness in her teaching and choreography. She reported extensive readings in Freud, Jung, and Reich and believed that this reading had somehow influenced her choreography and her teaching.

Interview 2—October 24, 2000 and January 15, 2001. I actually interviewed participant #2 twice. The first interview took place in my office on October 24, 2000. However, the defective tape recorder did not capture the majority of the interview; the transcriber could retrieve only four pages of the conversation. The researcher was faced with the question of whether or not to keep the interview as a part of this study. After a consultation with the committee chair, Tom Greening, Ph.D., Interview participant #2 was notified of the dilemma, and a second interview was requested.

The second interview was conducted by telephone on January 15, 2001, and the transcription was made once again. The final interview transcript is 17 pages in length, and is a combination of both interviews.

> Interview participant #2 has been described as a contemporary experimental dancer....Her choreography, which is staged by her own troupe, as well as the Limón Dance Company and others, is often described as postmodern. Many pieces contain violence, and human beings are depicted as trapped by powerful modern forces that they do not necessarily recognize. (Raugust, 1998, p.453)

Interview participant #2 was born in 1933 and graduated from Prospect Heights High School in Brooklyn, New York. She took her first dance lesson when she was 8 years old. She recollected,

> I was one of those children who always danced, and I was sort of a little annoying to my mother. And she took me to a psychologist and said...his name was Dr. Lieber..."What do I do with my daughter? She hasn't stopped twirling." And he said: "Give her dancing lessons." And that's when it all began....The first dancing school was Miss Bea's Dancing School. It was in Brooklyn. [Participant #2, p.1]

When the school encouraged her parents to increase the number of dance classes, they took her to the Henry Street Settlement Playhouse on the Lower East Side. She received a scholarship at the school there when she was 13 years old. In 1948, Alwin Nikolais became the director of the Playhouse school. Because Alwin Nikolais, his school and his choreography, had a profound impact upon 2 members of this research study, it is important to highlight him briefly.

Alwin Nikolais is a theatrical magician, a magus of movements conceived of in a pictorial fashion. He has effected a style of dance that draws on the technical resources of the theater....He refuses to be bound by the concerns of the dance audience that demands emotionally charged and linearly developed stories. The kinetic impulse of dance is subsumed in his work into the ordering requirements of visual design. (McDonagh, 1970, p.206)

Nikolais is portrayed as an innovative choreographer who broke the forms that had been characteristic of American modern dance. He began to study dance when he was 23 years old; during the 1930s he studied at the Bennington Summer Festival during the summers. Working with composers like Riegger, Honneger, and Prokofiev, Nikolais choreographed dances that reflected his social concerns. (McDonagh, 1970, pp.208-209).

After his Army service during World War II, " he returned to Hartford to stage…dance works he had created in a summer at Colorado College when Hanya Holm ran a summer course. Nikolais had studied with her earlier and was an admirer of her work" (McDonagh, 1970, p.210).

In 1948, Nikolais was invited to become the director of the Henry Street Playhouse in New York City. In addition to renovating the physical facilities, he reorganized the administration of the Playhouse. He also initiated a children's performing group and created a complete program of dance education. Alwin Nikolais shifted the entire field of modern dance in a significant way.

At Henry Street, he did away with the Freudian symbols and began to concentrate on movement, not as mime representation of characterization or universal archetypes, but for its own sake. He worked on improvisation classes with his students and began to strip away the layers of training that he himself had received in the search for bodies that were "clean" and not stressed with the emotional tensions of traditional modern dance.

(McDonagh, 1970, p.211)

Nikolais was a revolutionary figure in the history of American modern dance. His role was similar to that of the humanistic psychologists: they also rejected Freudian rigidity and reductionism and then affirmed the human potential to be authentic and personally expressive. He shifted the vision of dance from the ideals of the previous generation, just as Martha Graham, Helen Tamiris, Jose Limón, Doris Humphrey, Charles Weidman, and Hanya Holm had done before him. His impact upon the world of modern dance is reflected in this study by research participants #2 and #4. These two dancer/choreographers studied at The Playhouse with Nikolais and performed together for the next 20 years. They each formed their own companies, and they continue to choreograph and remain professionally active.

Interview participant #2 described the dance program at the Henry Street Playhouse, which had been initiated by Nikolais. "We studied dance technique, improvisation, choreography, percussion, notation, and stagecraft" [Participant #2, p.2]. She also studied modern dance with Merce Cunningham, Zena Rommett, took jazz with Luigi, and ballet classes with Robert Joffrey, William Griffith, Lillian Moore, Beatrice Tompkins, and Edward Caton [Participant #2, p.3].

When questioned about her connections to the Jacob's Pillow dance festival, she replied that she had gone there to dance with the Murray Louis dance company. She also spoke fondly of Ted Shawn and reminisced about meeting him for the first time at The Pillow.

> I remember Papa Shawn, Ted Shawn, he was quite wonderful....We were in this studio rehearsing. And the studio was filled with photographs....And I was in there with Murray Louis. I think there were two doors. I think he entered at one door, came through, and exited another. And he walked us through, he stopped and I remember I think he hugged Murray. And we all stopped in awe. He welcomed us. And he

explained the holy ground that we were rehearsing on and in reference to that studio where so many people have rehearsed. And he made references to the photographs. And it was just lovely. And then he just left. [Participant #2, p.5]

This statement illustrates how Ted Shawn promoted the mystique of Jacob's Pillow, as he welcomed this dance company. Participant #2 voiced additional thoughts about Jacob's Pillow that were less positive. She spoke at some length about the politics involved in the selection of the dance companies that were invited to perform on The Pillow stages (there are now three performance areas at Jacob's Pillow, the Ted Shawn Theater, the Doris Duke Theater, and Inside Out).

My company was formed in 1970....So, I had no reason to dance at The Pillow prior to 1970, other than my working with other companies. But during the time when I had a company...I was pushing to get booked....It was during the time when if you were a paradigm, if you were associated with a school or something, there was a very big backlash and post modernism came in. And it was quite strong in the late '70s. I think whoever was in charge at that time didn't...think that my company or my work was something they wanted at Jacob's Pillow. [Participant #2, pp.4-5]

This participant was one of two research participants to reflect upon the experience of not being invited to perform at Jacob's Pillow (see interview with Participant #3). However, during the 1970s, this research participant was successful in many other ways. "In the 1970's, [she] became popular, got her first CAP'S [Creative Arts Public Service Programs] grant, started getting grants from the New York State Council on the Arts, and the National Endowment, [and] in 1974 received a Guggenheim" (Jowitt, 1985, p.290).

This participant was regretful about not performing with her company at Jacob's Pillow but expressed no bitterness. Instead, she continued the interview by describing a memorable experience she'd had watching Ruth St. Denis perform at the Henry Street Playhouse. The participant recalled,

> It was in the 1950s that...Nikolais let her have the Henry Street Playhouse....She filmed *White Jade* and she filmed a couple of other things. And we knew that she was on the premises....And there was this teacher upside down, with all her wrinkles really like coming down on her head, just meditating. Standing on her head. And we just had a fit....Nik [Nikolais] had asked her, would she give a performance for the Saturday Children's Series...that was free of charge....And she consented to do that....We were in the audience and there was the neighborhood children, the house was filled....

> The curtain opened up. And there was Miss Ruth on a pedestal, looking so ravishing....We were awestruck. And the kids said – it went through the whole house—It's God, it's God!

> That's the transformation. It was amazing....It said everything about a woman's transcendency. It said everything about theater. And it was just wonderful....Her powers were extraordinary. [Participant #2, pp.6-8]

Participant #2 said that she had been about 17 years old at the time of St. Denis's performance at the Henry Street Playhouse. Her enthusiastic recounting of this story seemed to make it just as fresh and alive for her as on the day it occurred.

Participant #2 was quite clear about her lack of interest in psychology. Her comment about this was explicit:

> Yeah, I don't read any. I think I was pretty close-mouthed when I spoke to

you [on October 24] because I really wasn't interested. I was brought up, if you have an itch, don't scratch, get rid of it. And after that first critical juncture, I realized that's exactly what I did. [Participant #2, p.13]

However, she had previously stated in the October 24th interview that she thought that "the world is very cluttered, and I think people need to clear their minds...any help anybody can get to put them in a positive mind is really useful" (Participant #2, p.11).

She went on to relate a story from her life. When she was 21, her parents had taken her to see a psychiatrist, because of her "wild behaviors." She saw Dr. Ruth Bucholz for two weeks, because in addition to

"Sowing my oats"...I wanted to move out of my [parents] house...I made a critical juncture then. I didn't understand what critical junctures were at that time, and she, [Dr. Bucholz] said, if you could understand them, then you know when you reach a critical juncture you have to move forward, hopefully. [Participant #2, pp.12-13]

It is relevant to note that this research participant had the help of a psychotherapist at two critical junctures. This first was as a small child, when her mother was advised to "give her dancing lessons." Although she may not be interested in reading about psychology, forms of psychotherapy that affirmed her authentic self-expressiveness had an important impact upon the course of her life and the development of her career.

Participant #2 spoke at length about several other matters of relevance to her. She stated that art had been extremely important to her throughout her life.

I am more involved with the art world in my inspiration.... Everything in life is an influence on me...Over the years, the way other artists express themselves influences me.... The value, some of the theory or theoretical principles that I was brought up on in terms of dance and composition are similar to those that are practiced in art. [Participant #2, pp.10-11]

She also reflected upon being a dancer:

I must say, I'm one of the few people that if asked, 'would you do it over again?' I would say, 'yes, exactly the same way'...but I would like to be an ice skater, to glide instead of dance barefoot. [Participant #2, p.14]

And when asked, what she enjoyed most about being a dancer, she responded,

I really enjoy creating, the moment of creation in the studio; it's very exciting, very full, and very interesting. I find that I am really working at the maximum of all my facilities [faculties?]. Performing is wonderful. I love performance; being able to make a connection with people and to have them respond. [Participant #2, p.15)

The final section of this interview deals with Participant #2's newest professional interest. She stated,

I don't produce in New York anymore. I'm doing something now that's really important. The Joyce Theater has a program that choreographers can apply to have choreographic advisors or mentors....to work with choreographers to aid them in fulfilling and honing their work, guiding them at this moment in time. It's a wonderful program that they have. And three choreographers asked for me this year....I've been working with three diverse choreographers. [Participant #2, p.17]

Participant #2 has continued to choreograph new works, and has become very involved in this new mentoring program at the Joyce Theater. She apparently continues to enjoy the life of a dancer/choreographer, even though she is no longer appearing on stage.

The major themes in this interview were the following: Participant #2's dance training and her many teachers and her on-going commitment to teaching, creating, and mentoring other choreographers. Although she had performed at Jacob's Pillow, she felt little connection to the festival, and had little interest in the historical site. However, she had strong positive memories of Ted Shawn and Ruth St. Denis. She was not particularly interested in psychology, or in reading psychology books. However, she did volunteer that two psychotherapeutic experiences had been highly significant to her during her earlier years. Finally, she felt that her study of art (in high school) had made art an essential part of her life, and of her creative process.

Interview #3—October 25, 2000. This interview was conducted by telephone and is unique in many ways. The participant is a member of the Pilobolus Dance Company, which has been described as follows:

> The creative method of Pilobolus is as remarkable as its prolific output. Working in an intensive, improvisatory manner, the company creates work collectively, with each dancer serving as one of the several choreographers for the group work. This distinctive method of collaboration diverges sharply from prevalent choreographic practice, as it provides dancers with a rare investment in movement patterns and theme. (DeFrantz, 1998, p.632)

The Pilobolus Dance Company reflects at least three types of rebelliousness in the field of modern dance. First, the original members were not dancers and had studied little, if any dance. Second, the primary focus upon improvisation to create dances is most unusual. Third, the company as a whole choreographs all of the dances collaboratively.

In this interview, the themes of collaborative creativity arise strongly, as do the impact of psychology, and the connections to Jacob's Pillow Dance Festival. The interview subject stated clearly, "I never did study dance. I took one class with this woman, Alison, at college....We all took one class with her. So that's the extent of our [dance] study" [Participant #3, p.2]. Pilobolus began in a dance class at Dartmouth College in the 1970s. Alison Chase was teaching the class (she became a member of Pilobolus in 1973). Instead of teaching any formal style of dance, "She set us to making dances immediately. And the idea that we could simply find movement that was amusing to us and organize it in some fashion was appealing" [Participant #3, p.3].

The participant went on to discuss what the company does with these "found movement objects." He described a process of automatic writing that this group follows. When I reflected that other dance companies were much more bound by forms than the Pilobolus group, he said,

> We are in a sense bound by no forms....What happens is that people study dance. And that inevitably gives them a sense of what dance is. There is a sort of conceptual boundary there that guides and goads, but also controls and constrains. And I think that because no one ever told us what dance was, we were free to say that anything was dance. [Participant #3, pp.4-5]

Pilobolus is unique as a dance company because of the communal process that produces the dances. Bremser (1999) offered the following explanation:

> Every performer was also directly involved in the creation of choreography. Any work they appeared in they had in some way helped to develop. The fashion for communal living situations during this age was mirrored in the artistic process promoted by Pilobolus. (p.193)

The interviewee offered another explanation for the company's collaborative process, saying, "We collaborate with each other in a sense, going back to the beginning, because we were too scared to stand out by ourselves. We kind of hung onto each other for psychological as well as physical support" [Participant #3, p.15].

This comment presented a dominant theme in this interview, which is the motivation behind the collaborative process of the Pilobolus company. "I think that we look at what we do as a form of self-analysis. I think we're more Freudian in this regard....We like to work from our psychological responses to the world" [Participant #3, p.11].

To initiate the creative process, these company members go into the studio and begin to improvise. This represents a change in methodology, because most choreographers work from an idea, a story, or a piece of music. The major choreographers are described as coming into the studio ready to work, with the dance already partially formulated (Taper, 1996).

> We place the movement objects in proximity to each other and then we see how they vibrate when they're brought into contact....There's some sort of artifact of this period of time; something we lay down as a record or a map....It's beyond thinking. It's sort of subthinking....I think those dances become sort of interesting records of our social and psychological interaction in a certain period of time. [Participant #3, pp.12-13]

This comment opened up the subject of psychology, which was discussed at great length. The interviewee became quite expansive, as the themes of group process and creativity were explored. The participant gave me a brief synopsis of the authors he had read in psychology classes in college, including Erik Erikson, B. F. Skinner, Jean Piaget, and R. D. Laing. When asked directly about Abraham Maslow, Rollo May, Carl Rogers, and James Bugental, the interviewee recognized only the name of Rollo May but stated that he had not read any of his books.

However, the interviewee has had a variety of experiences with psychologists and psychiatrists. He discussed the fact that his son's Attention Deficit Disorder had precipitated his family into family therapy sessions. In addition, the entire Pilobolus company had worked with Salvatore Minuchin for a 2-year period. Dr. Minuchin had worked with them as a family group, and the participant believed that these psychotherapy sessions had been helpful to the company.

Salvatore Minuchin is a well-known family therapist whose educational background is relevant to this study. Minuchin wrote,

> Between 1954 and 1958 I was in training at the William Alanson White Institute in New York City, because I was attracted to the ideas of Harry Stack Sullivan....and to Erich Fromm, who saw man rooted in culture, and the other cultural psychologists like Karen Horney, Abraham Kardiner, and Erik Erikson. (Minuchin & Nichols, 1993, p.25)

Rollo May was a training analyst at the William Alanson White Institute during this period of time and had also been influenced by the neo-Freudians in the development of his ideas (Hoffman, 1999b).

Minuchin moved to Philadelphia in 1965 to become the director of the Philadelphia Child Guidance Clinic (Minuchin & Nichols, 1993, p.31). This particular clinic was a famous training facility for family therapists. In the 1930s, Otto Rank had been a speaker at the clinic, and his work was translated into English by Jessie Taft, a renowned social worker connected to this facility. Carl Rogers, in discussing the evolution of his client-centered counseling, stated, "Especially important are the roots of client-centered therapy to be found in the therapy of Rank, and the Philadelphia group, which has integrated his views into their own" (Rogers, 1951, p.4).

It therefore becomes possible to trace the influences through the generations: Otto Rank taught at the Philadelphia Child Guidance Clinic, and Carl Rogers acknowledged Rank above all others in the evolution of his work

(Hoffman, 1999b). In an interview in 1975, Rogers was asked, "Were you influenced by Rank?" Rogers responded,

> Yes, I was. I was not so much influenced by the setting of a time limit, but by many of his other ideas of the relationship and focusing more on the present. I was influenced primarily in an indirect way. Some people who had worked with the Philadelphia School of Social Work, which was quite Rankian in its orientation, had quite an impact on me and they got Rank to Rochester for a three day seminar, which was fruitful...I thought his therapy was very good. There's no doubt that my 'therapy' was influenced by his thinking. (Evans, 1975, p.29)

Salvatore Minuchin studied first at the William Alanson White Institute during Rollo May's tenure because of the attraction of the culturally oriented psychologists at the Institute. Minuchin then brought these ideas with him to the Philadelphia Child Guidance Clinic, where family therapy was taught and revered. The Pilobolus Dance Company experienced a form of family therapy with Salvatore Minuchin. It is possible to say that this participant (and his companions in the Pilobolus Dance Company) was affected by his work with the descendants of the four humanistic psychologists.

The final topic covered in the research protocol focused upon the research participant's connections to the Jacob's Pillow Dance Festival. Comparisons have been made between Pilobolus and Denishawn. Denishawn was the name of the Dance Company originated by Ruth St. Denis and Ted Shawn. Denishawn disbanded in 1930, which immediately preceded the purchase of the Jacob's Pillow site by Ted Shawn in 1931 (Owen, 1997a, p.6).

> In impact this small ensemble...recalls the popularity held by the St. Denis and Shawn enterprise in the 1920's. In kind, the mixed bills put on by Pilobolus are similar to the 'high-art' vaudeville fare of the Denishawn

troupe....Both aesthetics...can be said to center on the sensual projection resulting from the direct display of the dancer's body. (Bremser, 1999, p.192)

When asked about the connections between Pilobolus and Jacob's Pillow, the research participant reflected that the work of the company has never been highly revered by the administration at The Pillow (Participant #3, p.192). However, during the 1990s the company was invited to design a touring program to celebrate the 100th anniversary of Ted Shawn's birth. The interviewee described the process that had occurred:

> We looked at a lot of old tapes; we resurrected an early Shawn piece. And I put together a program with eight men dancers of contemporary...and some not so contemporary works for men....We put together a touring show, which toured for a couple of years as a sort of Jacob's Pillow men dancers. [Participant #3, p.6]

When I expressed surprise that Pilobolus had not found a more welcoming place at the Pillow Dance Festival, the research subject reflected a theme that occurred in many of the other interviews. The theme is the positive connection that so many dancers felt with Jacob's Pillow and the actual physical site on which The Pillow rests.

> It's a great little theater....We like the whole country vibe. Like Shawn, we have chosen to spend our lives outside of the geographic center of the movement world. We find the maples and the fox and migrating geese congenial....as Shawn did. [Participant #3, p.7]

I persevered with this theme, comparing Ted Shawn's choreography, which had utilized the motions of agriculture and carpentry as dance movements, with the work(s) of the Pilobolus company. Shawn's choreography for his company, the Men Dancers, had shifted the concept of dance into a new arena, as does the choreography of the Pilobolus company. The research participant responded,

> That's one of the reasons…we all felt when we were working on this Men Dancer project, [that] it was a harmonious fit. The piece we picked…to do was called *Kinetic Molpai*. And I thought it was very inventive, modern piece, really drawn from a process of invention.…I thought it was very freshly conceived. [Participant #3, p.8]

The Pilobolus company provides an interesting illustration from the contemporary dance world of connections between dancers and humanistically trained psychologists. And this particular company is also closely linked choreographically to Jacob's Pillow through their innovative choreographically and their presentation. The themes for Interview #3 include collective creativity, psychology and group process, and a substantial, multifaceted connection to the Jacob's Pillow Dance Festival.

Interview 4 —November 8, 2000. Participant #4 was 72 years old at the time of the interview, retired as a dancer, but still teaching and choreographing. This interview was conducted by telephone. Although he is currently living in Santa Fe, he returns to New York City four times each year to conduct the "Bessie" workshops at New York University. Bessie Schönberg was originally a dancer in the early Martha Graham Company. When a knee injury ended her career, she devoted herself to teaching, which she did until she died at the age of 90. Schönberg taught at Sarah Lawrence College from 1938, becoming head of the department in 1942, until she retired in 1975. After retiring from Sarah Lawrence, Schönberg taught at the Dance Theater of Harlem, the Juilliard School, New York University, Jacob's Pillow Dance Festival, the Dance Theatre Workshop, the London Contemporary Dance School and the American Dance

Festival. The "Bessie" awards are the New York Dance and Performance awards, which have been given annually by the Dance Theatre Workshop since 1984 (Marcotty, 1998, pp.701-702).

The interviewee began his dance training earlier than the other men in this study, taking tap lessons while still in grade school. His modern dance training began at the University of Wisconsin with Marge H'Doubler and Louise Kloepper. He spoke to me at length about H'Doubler.

> Her premise was never that she was going to make professional dancers. But she made more professional dancers probably than anybody else at that time. And she produced all kinds of the big educators that took over the departments and started departments across the country. [Participant #4, p.3]

While at Wisconsin, this research participant studied with Hanya Holm, who was teaching at Colorado Springs during the summers. He also attended the American Dance Festival in Connecticut. He connected the "very deep and penetrating experience" of his work with Marge H'Doubler to Holm's approach to teaching dance, and he decided to come to New York to continue his studies with Holm.

When he arrived in New York, he received a scholarship to study with Martha Graham. He stated that he had been unwilling to devote himself exclusively to that technique, and he had studied with several of the modern dance pioneers. *The International Dictionary of Modern Dance* (1998) noted that he had studied with "Helen Tamiris, and Doris Humphrey, and then went on to acclaim, dancing in their companies, and those of Anna Sokolow, Murray Louis, John Butler, Phyllis Lamhut, and Rod Alexander" (Raugust & Benet, 1998, p.665).

When this interviewee was asked about his knowledge of psychology, he described his experiences at great length. He stated that when he was in graduate school at the University of Wisconsin,

> We did the first work with movement therapy....I worked with Shirley
> [Guenther] and the graduate students at Mendota State Hospital. And in
> that process, I thought, 'My God, these people aren't far away from me.'
> So I started some analytic work there. [Participant #4, p.13]

In fact, this participant recalled that Marian Chace (the "mother" of dance/movement therapy: Hoffman, 1999c) had taught at the University of Wisconsin during the 1950s when he was a student there. He recalled reading some of her materials, as well as that of Joseph Moreno, who had been an originator of psychodrama, and had been one of Chace's teachers when she was working at St. Elizabeth's Hospital in Washington, DC during the 1940s (Hoffman, 1999c). This participant also cited Shirley Guenther as an important teacher in his life, who had introduced him to the work of Chace and Moreno, and to the books of Karen Horney and Erich Fromm.

This research participant spent many years of his life in psychotherapy. He described many therapists with whom he had worked, highlighting the depth-analysis (of 6 or 7 years) with a student of Theodore Reik (a nonmedical analyst who had studied with Sigmund Freud before immigrating to the United States), and his work in group therapy with Louis Ormont. (Dr. Louis Ormont studied with Dr. Reik, and worked for 25 years with Dr, Hyman Spotnitz, who developed major revisions of the original Freudian ideas and tenets. E-mail from the Ormont Organization, May 5, 2001.)

When questioned about the impact of his psychotherapeutic experiences upon his life and his professional work, the participant became quite articulate. He recalled a time when he had been studying acting with Irene Daley in New York City:

> Also my studying acting had a big influence on me, studying Stanislavski

[Constantin Stanislavski, writer of *My Life in Art,* was the originator of The Method technique in acting. His work had an impact upon many of the dancers in this study]....It all fit together with my dance experience at that time...in its approach to work,...working it through yourself. Also analysis at that time. I was in analysis, in and out during that whole period of development. And so they all fit together in terms of making dances, the resource is yourself. That's where you've got to come out from. [Participant #4, pp.19-20]

Participant #4 considered becoming an actor at one point during his life, but his therapeutic experiences influenced his choice of a career.

I seriously considered becoming an actor and not becoming a dancer. Or at least, giving up certain aspects of my dance. That was part of the transition. But that's not the way I swung. I went the other way. And went to dance because dance was what really fulfilled my life. [Participant #4, p.21]

Furthermore, his psychotherapy had been important to him because

It's all tied together. I can't separate the acting experience from the [Marge] H'Doubler experience, from the Hanya [Holm] experience from my performing experiences. They did all gel and come together....I was one of the lucky ones that did manage to put it all together. [Participant #4, p.25]

This research participant elected to discuss how important teaching dance has been to him and what a significant part it has played in his life. He stated that he loves to teach and has always enjoyed the feedback he has received from his students. Research participant #4 taught at Adelphi College for 10 years and at

Sarah Lawrence College for another 10 years. He then taught theater at the Juilliard School, composition at New York University, and went on to become a full professor at Rutgers University in New Jersey. He stressed the importance of being a dance teacher at a university.

> The halls of academia are the ones that have really made modern dance. It was the grounding of most of modern dance, the support of the colleges and universities. And I have always loved teaching at all of the schools...because it stimulates them [the students], but it also stimulates me as the teacher, to have to put things together, and organize them, and to try to get concepts across. [Participant #4, p.25]

His commitment to teaching has also been combined recently with his earlier work with Hanya Holm.

> In the 1970's, he [this participant] taught at Holm's studio and choreographed some of her final productions....In turn, [he] was responsible for the preservation of Holm's works...for Mikhail Baryshnikov's White Oak Dance Project in 1993 and 1994, and Holm's *Ratatat* for the 70th anniversary of Lathrop Hall at the University of Wisconsin in 1996. (Raugust & Benet, 1998, p.666)

It was striking to me that this renowned dancer/choreographer and experienced teacher felt so minimal a connection to the Jacob's Pillow Dance Festival. The Pillow school of dance was one of the earliest summer schools of modern dance in the United States, and the school continues to this day. Participant #4 stated clearly that he felt the actual experience of performing at The Pillow in the 1960s and 1970s had no impact upon his professional work. "No, I wouldn't say that I was influenced. I think I was more influenced by what Ted Shawn wrote, or looking at pictures, or knowing Barton Mumaw [one of the original Men Dancers]" [Participant #4, p.10].

This participant said that he was aware of the Jacob's Pillow concept, but he felt that the connections he made with the other dancers he encountered while in residence at The Pillow were the most significant to him. He reflected that Jacob's Pillow represented "a haven for dance...the primary places to study modern dance were Jacob's Pillow, the American Dance Festival or with Hanya in Colorado Springs" [Participant #4, p.11]

The major themes in the interview of participant #4 are the importance of his many teachers, the impact of his extensive involvement in psychotherapy, and his many years as a teacher of dance and theater. His relationship with the Jacob's Pillow Dance Festival was minimal, since he performed there, but he never studied or taught there. It was interesting to note that the psychotherapeutic experiences of this participant paralleled the evolution of psychotherapy itself. He began with a psychoanalytic experience, continued his work with a student of Theodore Reik (a lay analyst), and concluded in the 1960s with Louis Ormont, a specialist in group therapy.

Interview #5—November 9, 2000. Research participant #5 was 84 years old at the time of this interview. He was interviewed by telephone at his home in Tempe, Arizona. He began to study dance at the age of 19 while he was a student at the City of College of New York. He studied with many modern dance teachers, such as Rae Moses, Martha Graham, and Anna Sokolow. His ballet teachers were Mme. Anderson-Ivantzova and Nenette Charisse [Participant #5, pp.2-4]. He also studied acting with Miriam Goldina, Sanford Meisner, and Stella Adler over a 20-year period (Knight, 1998, p.570). These acting teachers were all proponents of The Method school of acting originated by Stanislavski. However, this participant believed that Helen Tamiris had been his most important teacher, as she had encouraged him to integrate his dancing with his acting skills.

When one dances, one is a whole human being; and so one is doing and acting. And she noticed that I had skill in acting and that I didn't know how to use that....And that opened up the whole world for me....I had skill as an actor, and I had a burgeoning skill as a dancer, which got a great lift when she opened that door for me. [Participant #5, p.4]

Interviewee #5 was in fact married to Helen Tamiris in 1946, and they formed their own dance company three years later. She died in 1966 (Knight, 1998, p.572). In this interview, this participant extolled the dancing abilities and choreographic talents of Helen Tamiris. He contrasted her work to that of Martha Graham, citing Tamiris as having presented the first modern dance concert in New York City.

Tamiris gave that first concert. And there she was, handling jazz material, American composers, and a modern movement....Her focus was America and what was happening in America, getting her movement from the life of America....And the whole impetus of movement, of moving from the torso was all a critical part of Tamiris' thinking. [Participant #5, pp.9-10]

This research participant took great pains to delineate the differences between the dance and choreography of Tamiris and Martha Graham. He extended this comparison by contrasting Graham's modern dance ballets with those inspired by the Denishawn style:

Denishawn was all caught up in Orientalia....Denishawn had a vaudeville sensibility. Denishawn didn't work from the gut, they did it from the mind, and the observation of how Indian dancers looked....They thought about how things looked. They also had a very naïve use of music. [Participant #5, p.9]

Martha Graham had been one of Denishawn's earliest students, and her break from them established a whole new approach to modern dance in America.

The decision to leave the Follies and Broadway with the aim of creating her own dance works broke the trajectory of Graham's Denishawn-influenced career. She was no longer an entertainer she was now something else—a dedicated artist. (McDonagh, 1973, p.45)

We then proceeded to discuss the Jacob's Pillow Dance Festival, which began after the partnership of Denishawn had terminated. This interviewee had performed at The Pillow three times, once with Helen Tamiris (1942), again in 1958, and in 1996 with jazz dancer Danny Buraczeski (Owen, 1997a, p.50).

Research participant #5 was highly ambivalent about Jacob's Pillow and what this Dance Festival had meant to him. When speaking of his first appearance at The Pillow in 1942, he said,

Oh it was very primitive. It was kind of fun....[We were] both awed and laughing at Shawn. And Miss Ruth was there....And Miss Ruth and Shawn sat there and told stories trying to top each other. And it was quite an experience. [Participant #5, p.10]

When I questioned him more specifically about the site of Jacob's Pillow, and how he had responded to that, he said:

Oh, it's lovely. I mean the only distraction is the grass growing....And it's focused. And everybody's on your side. And the food is sometimes terrible, but it becomes less important. No telephone. It's the kind of thing that artists have a hard time finding in America. [Participant #5, p.12]

As a final comment in the interview, the participant offered this statement: "Just specifically, Jacob's Pillow was a lovely experience; it had no profound effect on my life or my insights" [Participant #5, p.23].

However, participant #5 did recall his contacts with Barton Mumaw (and

Shawn) outside of the Jacob's Pillow venue. During World War II (in 1942), participant #5 and Barton Mumaw were both stationed at Keesler Field in Biloxi, Mississippi. The interviewee remembered,

> Barton would be teaching some things from Pilates [Joseph Pilates designed a series of strengthening exercises for dancers and he also taught at Jacob's Pillow]....And there are a couple of exercises that I remembered and I would do. Intellectually and ideologically, we were miles apart. I thought that he was a marvelous dancer....And years later, I taught him my solo in *Annie Get Your Gun,* and he toured in that dance. [Participant #5, pp.7-8]

This anecdote was repeated in the memoirs of Barton Mumaw, with a bittersweet twist to the tale.

> During my basic training days in the army, I had been surprised and delighted to discover that [Participant #5] was in my outfit....[He] was fully as accomplished a dancer as I, yet he seemed to have real respect for my work....I could have no idea that he would be instrumental in bringing me to *Annie Get Your Gun.* After his wife, Helen Tamiris, signed me on for the national company, [he] taught me the Indian dance, which he was performing nightly in Ethel Merman's New York Company. (Sherman & Mumaw, 2000, p.299)

The final series of questions in this interview focused upon psychology and psychotherapeutic experiences. The participant opened this discussion with the comment, "My original impetus was to be a psychiatrist or a psychiatric case worker. And I got derailed....I took a couple of dance lessons and was hooked" [Participant #5, p.13].

He assured me that he had done some reading in the field, but warned me not to ask him what books he had read. However, he later stated that "I won't tell you that I think Freud has the answer. Or that the behaviorists have the answer. I'm not of any particular school. I'm very suspicious of schools" [Participant #5, p.14].

Later in the interview, the participant stated that he had read some Freud and was also familiar with the works of the neo-Freudians, Karen Horney and Erich Fromm. He was unacquainted with the names of Abraham Maslow, Rollo May, Carl Rogers, and James Bugental.

He laughingly stated that he had

A couple of sessions with a Freudian lady. And I was then very well equipped to help all my friends through their problems....Because I got the whole language and I knew how to interpret dreams. I'm actually pretty good at it. I'm actually very good for instance at analyzing handwriting. Because handwriting is an action....Just like I can watch a person walk and tell you about them. [Participant #5, pp.14-15]

This interviewee also related that he had gone to the Payne Whitney Clinic in New York City, and worked with a therapist trainee for 6 visits. He stated "I got some real insights and thanked him and we left. And it was wonderful" [Participant #5, p.16]. He then discussed a recent experience, which had been painful and humiliating, and stated that he had become depressed. He described his epiphany in detail:

I was hurrying, getting ready to teach a class. And suddenly I did something very strange. I backed off from myself, and I looked at myself, and I said: "You're a very nice man. You're a decent human being. You do good work....You respect people and people respect you. Why the hell are you bugging yourself so much?....Why are you always criticizing yourself so much?"

And the strangest thing happened. I began to weep so bitterly that I was weeping like a child…you know, where kids when they cry too much they begin to gasp…. And it was one of the most important revelations of my life. Here I was…67. It's ridiculous.

I went back. I sat down at the typewriter….And I described the situation. And while I was typing, I was crying out loud. And I took off from there. I was fine. But what kills me…what gives me such a kick, is that I didn't have any professional help. [Participant #5, pp.19-20]

When this research participant was questioned about this experience, he was quite clear that he had experienced this as a real separation between different parts of himself, recalling that "I was three feet away, diagonally behind me, looking at this guy" [Participant #5, p.22]. This type of embodied dialogue between individual parts of the self and the Aware Ego, is a characteristic of the Voice Dialogue system of self-exploration (these techniques have been developed and explored by Hal and Sidra Stone, *Embracing Our Selves, The Voice Dialogue Manual,* 1989).

The research participant's comment about not having any professional help in this situation is reflective of his ambivalence about psychology and psychotherapy. His final reflection on this subject was that whenever "I'm in trouble, I write," [Participant #5, p.22]. He also discussed the challenges he currently faces; at 84 years of age with a hip replacement, he can no longer run and jump. He knows that there are many projects,

…10,000 things I could do. And none of them excite me very much. And something very strange has taken place….I can sit there and just be absolutely quiescent. I can just enjoy the stillness….So what I do when I'm in trouble is I write" [Participant #5, p.21].

The interview with participant #5 was difficult to evaluate. He became angry with me early in the interview (pp.4-5), because he felt that I should have known the answers to the historical questions in the protocol. In reviewing the transcript, I discovered that I did not provide an adequate explanation of how a research interview is conducted, with all of the participants being asked the same basic questions. How much of his irritation is reflected in the remainder of the interview is difficult to assess. He certainly expressed ambivalence about many people and many different things.

The primary theme that emerged from this interview was the participant's belief in the importance of his many teachers. He stressed the impact of Helen Tamiris (whom he did not identify as his former wife) and of his many acting instructors. He stressed his lack of psychotherapy and laughed at the language of the Freudians (which he claimed to have mastered after a few sessions). Although he warned me not to ask him about any specific readings in psychology, his subsequent discussion illustrated that he had considerable knowledge of the subject. His two experiences with psychotherapy were brief, and he was most proud of the work he had done for himself, without outside help.

This participant's reflections about the Jacob's Pillow Dance Festival were also ambivalent in nature. He stated that the festival had been interesting and enjoyable, although he thought that it had had no impact upon him or his professional work.

Interview #6—November 17, 2000. The interview with research participant #6 was conducted in person, in his office, which also houses his vast archives of photographs, programs, and memorabilia. This participant celebrated his 75th birthday in 2001, which fills him with great delight. This native New Yorker received his BS degree from New York University and was pleased to report that he has since been awarded two honorary doctorates, making him "a doctor, doctor, I love that" [Participant #6, p.7].

Well, I always danced. I was a natural....As a kid I always moved, always danced. I had no formal training until I got out of the army, and started studying with Nik [Alwin Nikolais] in 1949 [Participant #6, p.8].

He was discharged from the Navy in San Francisco, "where he studied acting, writing and dance with Ann (later Anna) Halprin. He worked in road company musicals and performed in a few night clubs" (Minderovic, 1998, p.499).

In 1949, this participant went to study at the Hanya Holm Summer School of dance in Colorado Springs.

I went to study with Hanya. She was doing a Broadway show, and Nik was taking over the school for the first two weeks I was there. She could not have done with this man's range, what he was doing to my mind. [Participant #6, p.10]

The participant was referring to Alwin Nikolais, and this meeting between the two men was serendipitous. The research participant followed Nikolais back to New York City, where he joined him at the Henry Street Playhouse. These two men created a legendary partnership, that lasted until Nikolais' death in 1993. During the interview, the research participant still reflected his sadness and loss at his colleague's death.

This interviewee was quite clear that Alwin Nikolais had been his most important teacher. When asked whether he had studied with anyone else after affiliating himself with Nikolais he stated,

My dear, I was worried that I would never have a life long enough to do all the things I wanted to do. It just began, and I was so busy I was just panicked that I would never live long enough to do everything. [Participant #6, p.11]

If Nikolais had been this participant's primary dance teacher, he also took the time to credit the rest of his dance lineage. When I discussed the legacy of Hanya Holm, he challenged me, reminding me about Mary Wigman: "She was Hanya's teacher. When you say that I'm from the family of Hanya Holm, no, it's really the family of Wigman" [Participant #6, p.3].

He displayed with great pride an original poster of Mary Wigman's first concert in Berlin in 1919. He then discussed Wigman's contributions to the field of modern dance:

> I think what her dancing did was, it opened up a wonderful trail....It's interesting that people like Nikolais who followed, emblazoned a trail...the way Mary did, in a different way....There was a very keen line in nothing but imagination and philosophy. It's antithetical to Nik's motivation. Yet what came out was the abstraction of it. It's the step beyond reality. The step into universality. [Participant #6, p.2]

The participant then moved the interview into the subject of teaching, which had been extremely important to him. In 1951, he became head of the children's dance department at the Henry Street Playhouse. "The children's performances were very popular, and at one time the ensemble was giving 150 performances per year" (Minderovic, 1998, p.498). The dance school at the Henry Street Playhouse was unique in many ways. It offered classes to the entire Lower East Side community, at very low fees. It also provided a full-time, intensive dance education to adult dancers who could afford to study full-time.

Interviewee #6 also took time out from his many responsibilities in New York to travel throughout the country as a guest teacher. "When interviewed, [his] students—children, adolescents, and adults—have all said not that he taught them 'how to dance,' but rather, that he showed them 'what dancing is all about'" (Harris, 1999, p.142).

Research participant #6 was so successful as a teacher and administrator that Ted Shawn offered him the directorship of the school at Jacob's Pillow. He recounted the story:

> I got to know Ted very well. Because he was being terribly ignored by the public at that time. But I saw the school in operation. I watched it. I saw it in the last year Ted was around, and his school taught this big variety and different range of movement....He offered me Jacob's Pillow School....Because we were having such success at the Playhouse...he wanted to have someone who knew how to run a school. His sessions were like twelve weeks. Who could take 12 weeks off? Who in a million years could do that? [Participant #6, pp.14-15]

This participant never taught at Jacob's Pillow but he (and his company) performed there six times between 1965 and 1979 (Owen, 1997a, pp.47-48). When asked about his experiences at The Pillow, he reminisced,

> I loved it....I'd be bundled up to my teeth because it was so cold on that stage there. It was piney and woody and smelled so good....It never influenced me. The only thing I enjoyed was the ambiance of the place. And Barton [Mumaw] and I got on like a house on fire. We became very close, and he danced, and he did so beautifully. There was such a kinship between us. [Participant #6, pp.13-15]

I wondered about the participant's knowledge of The Pillow site and its historical background. He explained how he had gotten to know all about the history of building of Jacob's Pillow and how Ted Shawn and his Men Dancers had literally built the first buildings. "That just indicates what a strong presence Shawn was there in the early days" [Participant #6, p.18].

This participant also had fond memories of staying at High Folly, an off-grounds guesthouse where visiting dancers were housed.

I met wonderful people on each program. We shared programs most of the time....He [Ted Shawn] always balanced his program. There was an ethnic, and a ballet, and a modern work....We lived off-campus. And we'd go back there and dinner would be ready for us. We would serve it ourselves....All the three companies, which was the soloist, and the two companies; and we would meet and have a communal dinner every night. It was wonderful....It was the kitchen. It was the warmth....And it forced us all to mingle and know each other. And we ate with each other. We had wonderful times. I loved High Folly. It burned down, I was told. [Participant #6, p.17]

The final series of questions in the research protocol dealt with psychology, psychologists, and the psychotherapeutic experiences. Once again, this participant was quite articulate on this subject.

I think that there is a philosophy, and there is a psychology, and a philosophy is the same as a psychology to me....I don't separate any of it....I'm totally familiar with the German, Swiss psychologists...like Jung, Adler, and Freud. [Participant #6, p.20]

After an interruption for coffee, brought to him at regular intervals by an assistant, this interviewee continued discussing his ideas about psychology. In response to a question about the neo-Freudians, specifically Erich Fromm, he replied,

I never read him. By then, I stopped reading....He wrote such long books. Whatever he had to say, he could say it in 6 pages, and there he goes, taking 600 pages. That was my theory about philosophical writing, and so I had no patience...The only person who I thought was the most lucid, the greatest psychologist-philosopher, was William James, who started the first school of psychology at Harvard. [Participant #6, p.23]

This research participant offered an enlightening historical perspective on the influence of psychology; it was also a viewpoint that had been expressed by other participants in this study.

At one time, Freudian psychology was so popular that it became a terror of the civilized world. You couldn't do anything that didn't have a Freudian interpretation. And it was ludicrous. It became a great point for satire, by everybody who…satirized the Freudian sexual psychology of life and the symbolism….Before the war, in the '30s, when things were a little calm, everyone went to see a psychiatrist….It was like a fashionable thing you did. It was in the '60s, when everybody, simply everybody had to have a shrink. They would not do a thing without that shrink….That to me meant nothing, but at least they were trying to get on with their life. But I couldn't get over [that] people had to be so dependent….But I saw through it. [Participant #6, pp.20-21]

Once again, a research participant in this study reflected knowledge of how psychology and psychotherapeutic practice had changed during the years from 1930 to 1960. He went on to offer his own views of his personal psychology. Referring to his book *Inside Dance* (1980), he stated,

It deals with how psychology within a person is not one part of me; my psychology is the me. And the other factors have different psychologies.

And very often, I would stop in choreographing and I'd say to the dancer, "Do you think that's possible?" And they would say, "Yeah, but you've got to get a better dancer than that. They're never going to do that." And I'd say, "Yeah…if I got someone else, do you think that movement could work if I swing it around that way?" "Oh sure, anybody with any talent could do that." I would get this back talk. The dialogue would be terrific.

And then the teacher in me would say, "Oh yeah, but be careful....You could injure yourself so easily with a movement like that. You could put that kid out of business." And the dancer would say, "Eh, to hell with it. If they want to be a dancer, they've got to face those kind of risks."

And I'd sit in the middle of this dialogue. But I'd come to a conclusion, or maybe they would come to a conclusion. [Participant #6, p.6]

This participant was also clear about how he would arrive at a decision when this type of dialogue between his several selves was in progress. He stated that he would have to make the decision in favor of the one who was using the body. And he assured me that this specific self (the embodied self) was not the "ego me. The ego me is very happy, go-lucky. I love food, I garden. Just don't bug me with all of this junk" [Participant #6, p.7].

Once again, I discovered that a participant had been personally involved in a type of dialogue between his different personalities. He was clearly quite comfortable with this process and had experienced it frequently during his professional work. This dialoguing process between an individual's "sub-personalities," with a separate part of the self, the Aware Ego, making the decisions, is foundational to the Voice Dialogue process (Stone & Stone, 1989).

To summarize, this research participant believed that his most important teacher had been Alwin Nikolais, stressing their subsequent professional affiliation at the Henry Street Settlement Playhouse. He was deeply involved as a teacher and became the director of the school of dance at the Playhouse. His extensive monologues emphasized how much he enjoyed the didactic role he was playing. This participant had many happy memories of his performances at Jacob's Pillow and the surrounding environment. He had also taken the time to learn all about the historical background of The Pillow. In fact, his success as a teacher and director of the school in New York City led Ted Shawn to offer him the directorship of the summer school at Jacob's Pillow. However, this interviewee stated that he had not been influenced by his experiences at The Pillow.

Although this participant denied any connection to the field of psychology, his comments indicated that he was familiar with various aspects of the field. He also reflected an awareness of the evolution of the psychotherapeutic process. He was also very willing to discuss his experiences in dialoguing with his various selves in a way that was quite contemporary.

Interview #7—December 1, 2000. Participant #7 was 64 years old at the time of the interview. She is a graduate of Mills College in California. She is a prolific choreographer and has been the recipient of many honors and awards, including two honorary doctorate degrees. She did not mention any of these awards to this interviewer, preferring to focus upon her work.

She revealed that she had studied with many of the famous names in the world of modern dance during her three summers studying at Connecticut College. However, when asked who her most important teachers were, she stated:

> Well, I was captured by dance when I was a child, which was Marian Ajgeage…. So that I had a powerful dose of the stage there and a powerful dose of improvisation from her and a relation to music. She was a pianist….Because if she hadn't existed in my life, I never would have found dance. [Participant #7, p.6]

She also cited two of her teachers at Mills College: Louis Horst, "because he was the key to my compositional development" [Participant #7, p.4], and Doris Dennyson, who was her music teacher. Dennyson had been a part of the first John Cage percussion ensemble.

Participant #7 had studied with Merce Cunningham, Alwin Nikolais, and Murray Louis at Connecticut College. She revealed that in 1960, she had been teaching improvisation at Reed College, and

> I didn't know anything about it. So I decided I better get myself to school.... I did go back to a summer workshop with [Anna] Halprin...for two years...and that's where I met all the legendary Judson people. Not all of them, but Yvonne Rainer and Simone Forti. And June Eckman was there.... [Participant #7, p.10]

These encounters with the pioneers of the Judson Church Theatre group proved to be significant for this participant's career. They introduced her to the notion

> ...of non abusive dance training....I know what it [this phrase] meant in that time. There was a real aesthetic and body-friendly notion that ballet and some modern dance companies were engaged in the heroics of dancing and not in a more humanistic kind of dancing....That is, if you lift your arm to the side, you didn't go through angst and grit and flew to get there. You just went straight to where you wanted to go with what it took to get there....It's not only the physical heroics but it's the dramatic heroics. Some sort of yearning and emotional purging that went on to stage right. That horrible stuff. [Participant #7, pp.11-12]

This research participant became a part of the Judson Church Dance Theatre and is one of the leading post-modernist dancers that developed from the Judson collective. She discussed the beginnings of this group. Upon the recommendation of Simone Forti and Yvonne Rainer, she had traveled to New York City and took a choreography workshop from Robert Dunn.

> He was an accompanist in the [Merce] Cunningham studio. He was married to Judith Dunn, who was in Merce's first company....And Bob

[Dunn] took the legendary music composition class that John Cage taught at The New School [for Social Research]. And John [Cage] asked Bob to transpose the information from music to dance, and to teach a dance class based on his principles. And that he did. And those classes disassembled major stereotypes in modern dance and led to the Judson Church Dance Theatre. [Participant #7, p.11]

Reviewing the evolution of this group of post-modernist dancers, dance critic Jack Anderson wrote,

By 1962, workshop members had created a body of pieces....They sought a space in which to present them. Two sympathetic pastors offered them the Judson Memorial Church, a congregation affiliated with both the Baptist Church and the United Church of Christ. Designed by Stanford White in Romanesque Revival style in 1892, the Church had long been active in the life of Greenwich Village. Howard Moody and Al Carmines, its ministers during the heyday of the Judson Dance Theatre, were known for their devotion to social issues and for their love of the theatrical arts. (Anderson, 1997, pp.219-220)

The noted musician, Steve Reich (1973), commented upon the post-modernist movement in American modern dance. He stated

The avant-garde dance of the 1960's focused on non-dance movements to be performed in concert situations. Walking, running, working with objects, and performing specific tasks were among the genuinely new alternatives to the modern dance of expressive movements of an earlier generation. The basic idea of the Judson dance group...could be summed up as; any movement is dance. That is the precise equivalent to the basic idea of the composer John Cage: "any sound is music." (p.336)

134

It would be helpful to understand something about what post- modernism meant in the history of modern dance. Participant #7 discussed the assignments given in Bob Dunn's choreography class.

> But the assignments were not anything I had ever heard of in dance classes. They were like, make a 3 minute dance. "Yeah, okay, but what's it about?" And it was only about 3 minutes is what it was about. So determinacy was introduced, the rolling of the dice and...all those procedures that tells one what to do as a choreographer....But I remember there was great argumentation about what is dance? The criticism or assessment of the work...was based on what did you see? Not what did you think about what you saw? And one got more used to analysis of, what is there [rather than] what's supposed to be there? [Participant #7 , pp.14-15]

Participant #7 is an outstanding example of the post-modernist movement in American modern dance, and she represents this innovative viewpoint. With post-modernism, the face of modern dance shifted once again, as it had done during the Denishawn years, and then again during the years of Shawn's Men Dancers. The significance of these events is that they reflect the eras in which they occurred. The Denishawn years (1915-1931) reflected a time of change, of post World War I turmoil, and presented a glorified elaborate vision of modern dance. The Denishawn Company toured throughout the world, presenting lavish productions and offering a new version of what dance could be. Ted Shawn's Men Dancers (1933-1939) toured through the United States, becoming the first group of American men performing dances together. The choreography that Shawn designed for these dancers was often based upon the building and agricultural chores required to develop and maintain the original farm at Jacob's Pillow.

The post-modernist pioneers (1960-1970) eliminated the literary and emotional referents that had guided the originators of modern dance. The post-modernists reflected the rebelliousness that characterized much of the 1960s, and was echoed by changes in music, in art, and in psychology.

Participant #7 discussed her fascination with improvisation:

I was operating in the wilderness of improvisation and loving it after being over-academicized by Mills [College]. And those pieces were presented in Bob's [Dunn] class and got on some of the programs at Judson....

And in those days, improvisation was considered dog doo, even by Bob Dunn....They didn't understand the rigor in it and they had no respect for the intuitive forces of the body, especially in a woman's body.

I moved away from improvisation because I was heading towards the stage, and a responsibility to an audience for a certain product. And you can't do that with improvisation, especially if you're in a 2,000 seat house. [Participant #7, pp.17-18]

As Participant #7 learned more about the infinite possibilities of movement, she also made a commitment to the development of dances that could be reproduced and seen (if not always understood) by her audiences. Many dance reviewers have discussed her work in its various phases. However, the review below captures both the qualities of her choreography, and her ceaseless inquiry into the forms of dance.

[Her] dances are shaped by dreams of levitation, by geometry, enigma, physics, by memory, mathematics and geography. Her gestural imagery challenges perception of the moving body, making the impossible appear possible....[She] makes the rules of life seem arbitrary, offering an exhilarating transcendence of physical limits. Since 1962, her choreography has explored the interplay of intellect and instinct, paradoxes of logic and non sequitur, interpenetrations of present and past, coincidences of abstract form and mythic action, and the edges between visibility and invisibility. (Goldberg, 1999, p.37)

This review captures a considerable amount of the quality of this highly intelligent, abstractionist choreographer. She is always challenging the observer to rethink and reconsider the rules of modern dance.

When the interviewer began to ask questions about Jacob's Pillow, the participant stated that she'd performed at The Pillow many times. Her first appearance was in 1980, and she recalled that Liz Thompson had been the director of the Jacob's Pillow Dance Festival at that time. During the time that her company was performing at The Pillow, Participant #7 taught classes at the summer school. She reflected that "I get inspired at certain places...I teach composition and I lecture about my work" [Participant #7, p.21].

Recalling her times in residence at The Pillow, she said:

In the early years, anything that came to me, that supported my company and my work went straight into my hall of fame....And just to be out of the city. I'm a nature girl and rarely see it. I don't know if it's there anymore.

And also Liz worked on the diet when she was there, and there was very fine vegetarian food.

So it was my work....it supported the company to work. And more recently...Ella Baff [the current director of Jacob's Pillow] funded in part the commissioning of the first of the jazz pieces, which by the end there were three. And so they [the pieces of choreography] come into being. [Participant #7, pp.21-22]

Participant #7 also praised The Pillow for its "outreach to the international community of dancers" [Participant #7, p.22]. She expanded this statement into a dialogue about her work in Europe, particularly in France. She and her company have been invited to teach on a yearly basis since 1973.

> Basically, my work was commissioned there. A studio of one's own and a stipend was forthcoming....What they did was systematically import American modern dance....And they wanted to know what it was. And they found out what it was in the most clever, most efficient way. They invited us to teach for long periods of time [Participant #7, p.24].

She summarized this discussion with her feelings of regret that French modern dance is so rarely seen and appreciated in the United States.

The final phase of the interview with this participant was focused upon the subjects of psychology and psychotherapy. Like many of the dancers interviewed for this study, she stated that she had read Freud while in school and little else since that time. She volunteered that she was familiar with the work of "a man operating with Anna Halprin...yes, Fritz Perls....I didn't study with him. And Laura Perls here in New York" [Participant #7, p.26].

However, she had not read of any of F. C. " Fritz" Perls' work, nor had she read any of the books of the four founders of humanistic psychology. She appeared to be familiar with the work of Laura Perls. She volunteered that because she had been at Mills College, she had been close to Esalen. However, she could not recall which workshops she had actually attended at Esalen.

This participant recalled that she had been familiar with "these people," meaning Halprin and Perls. However, she stated that

> I remember being somewhat perplexed by Anna's incorporation of psychology in her work. I found it curious. I was involved in the Judson aesthetic, which was debunking narrative and emotion and character and

psychology. So I found her direction in community work and ritual in the end justified her research. But at the time that she was doing that research, I didn't know where it was going. [Participant #7, pp.27-28]

Participant #7 will be known historically as one of the great innovators in the field of modern dance. However the quote above reveals the respectfulness with which she can observe the work of another dancer/choreographer who is working from a different viewpoint.

She was asked if she had any experiences with psychotherapy, and if so, had this had any impact upon her work. She replied that she had "put in some years in psychotherapy....I don't know what [type of therapy] it was. It was not Freudian. It was very, very helpful" [Participant #7, p.32].

When questioned further about whether her psychotherapy had fed into the development of her professional work, had nourished it or supported it, she responded:

Well, it had to have, because it's part of the writing of [her name]....I do know that my work is autobiographical. It can't help but be....I mean, once you dump early modern dance, what do you replace it with? I didn't replace it with what [Merce] Cunningham replaced it with. I've had to invent that. So you invent yourself. [Participant #7, pp.31-32]

She also thought that there had been great empowerment that came from this particular psychiatrist. He had said to her,

"You have to remember that I grew up before women's liberation....And to step out and take a place requires some kind of rewriting of one's background." And that had to have empowered the work that I did. And other things have empowered it. I'm just constantly talking to myself. Just: "What do you think, dear? We know that now. Trust yourself."

[Participant #7, pp.33-34]

Participant #7 expressed not only her positive feelings about her therapist, but she also understood the importance of the psychotherapeutic experience upon herself and upon her professional work. Once again, a research participant discussed the process of dialoguing between a subpersonality and her Aware Ego. In her case, the process appears to be both comfortable for her and comforting as well.

This research participant also discussed the visual arts, and stressed their impact upon her work.

I wanted to tell you, there's a component in my being that is not very often included in the understanding of a choreographer. But I was very influenced by the visual art world. I was a participant....They [other visual artists] saw my suspended structure...and it affected their paintings and their sculpture. I was in that mix. And I drew all through those years. And especially in 1975, I drew a grid...in a piece called *Locus*. But it was graphing this immediate space around my body, that gave me the dance that I have. And I still do it to this day. It's kind of a mantra.

So a lot of my compositional use of the stage is informed from that aspect of my work. I'm very close with...many, many artists....Usually my friendships have embraced people who work in sculpture as well as painting.

I have a different system of selecting gesture than anyone else I know. And it's an evolving vocabulary.

When I went back into dance, I worked on structure. I foregrounded structure in my work....That was the accumulation of all these mathematic systems for organizing material.

There's a paradox in...my movement vocabulary. One, it's very finely etched in the geometrics of my visual arts side. And also, the counterpoint to that is a more organic kind of movement, the sequential, multidirectional stuff....And those two things come up against each other. And I like the difficulties of transitioning from one to the other. The sort of grit, the sparks that fly when you do that [Participant #7, pp.29-32].

This long statement is included because it permits this highly articulate participant to discuss her choreographic methods at length, and it provides an excellent summary statement for this interview.

The predominant themes for interview #7 were many. First, there were her many teachers, not just of dance, but of music and of compositional forms. This exposure led to her personal development as one of the leading post-modernist choreographers. She also stressed her ongoing connection to the world of the visual arts, which impacts many aspects of her professional work.

Another important theme in this interview was the impact of her years in psychotherapy, which she believed was empowering for her and has assisted her in the creation of her essentially autobiographical works.

Participant #7 stressed the importance of the ongoing support she had received from the directors of the Jacob's Pillow Dance Festival. She also commended The Pillow for its support of European modern dance (and dancers). She expressed great appreciation for the extensive financial support she and her work had received from the French government.

Interview #8—December 16, 2000. Research Participant #8 was 61 years old at the time of the interviews and was teaching at the Boston Conservatory of Music. She was a principal dancer in the José Limón Dance Company for 21 years. She has taught at the Juilliard School, Manhattanville School, American University (Washington, DC), Skidmore College, and Bennington College.

There has been almost nothing written about Participant #8: an extensive archival search of the Dance Research Collection of The New York Public Library revealed no reviews, interviews, or articles about her. There are many videotapes of her in performance with the company. There were four clippings in her file, all of which show her dancing, but do not discuss her as a performer. I obtained access to the archives of The Limón Foundation, and found two newspaper articles. These are dated April 1, 1975, and they describe Participant #8's accident onstage, during the dance *Brandenberg Concerto #4*. The following information came from a biography, prepared for publicity purposes by The Limón Foundation.

> She teaches the Alexander Technique both privately and for groups of special interest....She is employed by the Limón Foundation as reconstructor of the Limón repertory and as a master teacher of the Humphrey/Limón technique. As such, she has reconstructed Limón works for many companies, including the Paris Opera Ballet, Joffrey Ballet, Les Grand Ballets Canadians, the National Ballet of Portugal, English National Ballet, and the Royal Swedish Ballet. (Limón Foundation)

When asked where she had been educated and what schools she had attended, Research Participant #8 responded, "I don't think I've been educated yet, except through dance. High school was in Westfield, Massachusetts...then I spent just two years at the Juilliard School, and that's it" [Participant #8, pp.3-4].

She began to study dance when she was six years old, taking classes in tap, ballet, and acrobatics at a local dancing school (in Westfield). When her mother was told that this participant was a talented dancer, she began to make inquiries.

> My mother was aware. She was a reader. And she knew about Jacob's Pillow, so this is pivotal in my life. And so she made an appointment to have me dance for Miss Craske [Margaret Craske was one of the foremost ballet teachers in the world, and in fact, many of the research participants studied with her]....She must have been horrified. Because indeed I performed my little recital piece on point with bent knees. She didn't let

me finish, but said, "Oh, thank you, dear."

But she made a big mistake also. You know how adults speak about children as if they don't exist? Psychologically it's very detrimental, and I suffered from it the rest of my life. She said: "For God's sake, now don't ever send her back there. In fact, it's probably too late. She's ruined. She'll never be able to dance" [Participant #8, pp.6-7].

This participant went on to study at several local schools near her home. She reflected, "Not until I went to Jacob's Pillow, when I was in high school, was the first time I ever had any real training" (Participant #8, p.8).

The Jacob's Pillow Dance Festival is renowned for the scope of its school and the expertise of its teachers. It is called The University of the Dance, and runs for 9 weeks each summer, paralleling the Festival. Students may elect 3, 6, or 9 weeks of classes. "Daily ballet and modern classes were augmented by studies in composition, dance notation, Spanish, East Indian, mime, and other disciplines " (Owen, 1997a, p. 24).

This research participant studied at Jacob's Pillow for three summers, working with Ted Shawn, Margaret Craske, Alfredo Corvino, Carol Goya, Matteo, and Ann Hutchinson.

Ann Hutchinson was teaching Labanotation when she was at Jacob's Pillow, and has become famous for this work. The study of Labanotation became important to this research participant and also has significant historical relevance. Labanotation is a method of transcribing movement sequences and entire dances. It is based upon the system called "kinetography," which was developed by Rudolph von Laban (1971), and discussed in his book, *The Mastery of Movement.*

Historically, Laban's innovative work connected him to the pioneers of modern dance and dance/movement therapy. Irmgard Bartenieff founded the Effort/Shape Certification program at the Dance Notation Bureau in New York City in 1965. Bartenieff studied with Laban during the 1920s in Germany, and she stated, "I came from European modern dance...and from Laban. It was a time of changes—post World War I Expressionism...[Mary] Wigman. It was not just the aesthetic theories...but mathematics, rhythm...the nature of it" (Pierpont, 1980, p.90).

Ann Hutchinson's book (1970), *Labanotation, Kinetography Laban: The system for Recording Movement,* translated Laban's work into a contemporary system for the transcription of all forms of movement. It has been used as the basis for the Effort/Shape evaluation method employed by dance/movement therapists to evaluate the movement vocabulary of their clients.

Participant #8 worked closely with Ann Hutchinson for many years, beginning with their work at Jacob's Pillow.

> She took me under her wing. She became my mentor in a lot of ways. Being a child of not much confidence, particularly being told I'll never be a dancer, she thought I had an aptitude for notation. And I went back to The Pillow as a scholarship student for Labanotation....So I helped her, I don't think it was a big help, but she gives me credit [in Shawn's book] *Every Little Movement* [1963], when she made the book and put down Ted Shawn's work in a notation. I was sitting there scribbling away. And would go home with her and we'd talk about it and write it. [Participant #8, p.10]

Ann Hutchinson continued to work with Participant #8 in the years after Jacob's Pillow. Hutchinson wrote a book *Limón-Based Modern Dance Technique (1989).* This book featured a series of classes taught by Participant #8, and labanotated by Ann Hutchinson Guest. The introduction states,

> The material in this book was taught in March 1979 for one of A.H. Guest's Language of Dance Classes at the Teacher Training College of the Royal Academy of Dancing in London.

[Participant #8] was for many years a leading dancer in the José Limón Company, and was hailed in Russia as a ballerina of modern dance. Her sense of lyricism and great range of quality developed from her work with Limón, who was himself a protégé of Doris Humphrey and Charles Weidman, leaders in developing modern, contemporary dance in the USA. (Guest, 1989, p.iii)

Participant #8 believed that Jean Cébron had been her most important teacher at Jacob's Pillow. Cébron had choreographed a piece on the dance students, and Ted Shawn had liked it enough to present it to the public in a Saturday matinee. She reflected: "So I performed at Jacob's Pillow before I was ever trained. And let me tell you, in a solo called *Moment, Absolute Mon Verge*....And that's what I auditioned for Juilliard with" [Participant #8, p.11].

She recalled how Cébron had further helped to shape her career:

The way Juilliard was set up, you had to choose which modern style you wanted, with Limón or Graham....I had heard of Graham, but she was still a graham cracker as far as I was concerned, and I had never heard of Limón....So, I said to Jean [Cébron], "What do I do?" He said, "For you...Limón." So I go on my little checkbox, Limón. You know how things happen?...

Because he was absolutely right...I could no sooner have danced Graham at that point in my life than jump off a building....It was to me holier than thou and phony....Certainly Limón [technique] was like putting a glove on. It was just perfect for my body and soul

The reason I got into Juilliard...was that I had studied at The Pillow those summers. And the faculty at Juilliard at that time was Miss Craske, and Mr. Corvino, and José Limón....I knew that they knew me and they took me, and I still thought that they made a mistake. [Participant #8, pp.22-25]

We then discussed this participant's most important teachers at Juilliard, and she highlighted (in addition to José Limón) Lucas Hoving, Betty Jones, and Antony Tudor. She recalled that when Tudor had suggested to her class that they read *Zen in the Art of Archery* (Herrigel, 1971), she had run out and sat in an all night place,

> Because I started reading it...I just sat there...and I finished it. I think that's what led me to Alexander [technique], and all the rest, years later....There's a pivotal teacher for you. Just pointing me in the direction of how to learn, for what real learning was about. [Participant #8, pp.25-26]

Participant #8 was clear about the progression of her dance education and how each phase of it had led into the next phase. However, because Jacob's Pillow had been such an integral part of her education, we discussed what The Pillow had meant to her. She responded,

> I am basically a country girl at heart. My inspiration, my spiritual connections are through nature....But my spiritual connection is dance and nature. And there it was....But it was just the perfect place, nestled in the hills. I was freezing cold. It wasn't anywhere as developed as it is now....It was cold. It was rough. But there, you did what you did....You eat, sleep, drink, breathe dance. Particularly with Shawn preaching. [Participant #8, p.15]

Participant #8 expressed ambivalence toward Ted Shawn. She said,

> He was a strange man....Oh, Shawn was by far not perfect....He accomplished a lot. I give him all the credit in the world for being a tenacious believer, and look at what he established. But he was extremely

egotistical. [Participant #8, p.16]

She recounted a long story about how Ted Shawn required that all the scholarship students meet in the studio in the evenings. He would show all of his old films, and would "drone on about his life...and it was history" [Participant #8, p.17].

> And then you'd see him...give those curtain warmer speeches and he was wonderful....he took great pleasure in doing that. But he was also informative and he brought so many people into a new awarenesses and beautiful programs....It was his idea of diversity, of showing the classic and the modern and the ethnic in almost every program. It was a wonderful thing to build an audience for that kind of range of dance, that was unknown to so many people. So I can only give him credit. He was impossible. [Participant #8, p.18]

This research participant performed at Jacob's Pillow, first as a student, and then in 1974, with the José Limón Company. She subsequently returned to teach master classes in the Alexander Technique. Participant #8 performed with the José Limón Company between 1963 and 1984.

After leaving the Limón Company, she studied the Alexander technique for 3 years. She is currently teaching at the Boston Conservatory of Music, where she teaches Limón technique, Modern Pedagogy, Limón Repertory Class, and Alexander Technique. She also sees people privately for individual Alexander sessions. She stressed the importance of the Alexander training, both as a teacher and as a dancer.

> It was a way to...clearly communicate the things I was trying to communicate ...such as letting your body do it rather than making your body do it. It's Zen...You have to get out of your own way. And what's in your way are your habits of thinking. And your habits of thinking are

incarcerated in your muscles. [Participant #8, p.29]

Participant #8 discussed another aspect of the Alexander Technique later in the interview, when questioned about her psychotherapeutic experiences. She stated,

I think my whole therapy has been the Alexander [Technique]....It's not a therapy but it served the same self-revealing, getting in touch with more of your whole self. I might even be in a place [now] that I might even consider psychotherapy as an option. But I never would have as a...not that I was against it, I thought it was helpful for them and all that. But I would never. [Participant #8, p.35]

When questioned further about the Alexander work as a therapeutic intervention, Participant #8 became quite articulate:

You begin to make it possible to believe absolutely that you can alter who you are, how you are, by what you think. Form follows function. And you change your thoughts; your thoughts change the function, and the form changes. It's possible.

You understand yourself...as dancers by your kinesthetic sense. But if you're getting the same problems recurring all the time, then your kinesthetic sense isn't reliable. This is what Alexander discovered. And this is the whole basis of habit and how you break the habit....The mind/body isn't separate. That was the connection....And if you change your thoughts....And through understanding that, you are more empowered than you thought you were. [Participant #8, p.35-37]

Participant #8 believed that her studies of the Alexander work had made her a much better teacher. She described her work as an Alexander teacher/worker.

> It requires you to be in the moment. When you put your hands on, you're
> in this moment of this contact, and you're plugging in. You're not looking
> or trying to fix. You're not trying to manipulate anybody. And you can't
> manipulate yourself either. [Participant #8, p.41]

This research participant was describing a body therapy session that bears
a strong resemblance to many descriptions of a psychotherapy session; i.e., the
therapist is completely present in the moment with the client, the therapist is not
trying to fix the client, nor to be manipulative.

The final portion of this interview explored the participant's knowledge of
psychology. She said that she had never taken a psychology class, but had read
Gestalt Therapy Verbatim (1969) by Perls. She had read many books on
educating children, and was interested in education per se. She said that she had
read all of Shirley MacLaine's books, because the subject of reincarnation
interested her a lot. One might construe this as a connection, albeit distant, to
transpersonal psychology.

Research Participant #8 is the only member of this study who was actually
a student at the Jacob's Pillow School of Dance. This was pivotal in her life,
because her work there led her directly into her studies at the Juilliard School. It
was also at Jacob's Pillow that she first worked with Ann Hutchinson, who
became an important figure in the history of dance and dance/movement therapy.
This connection to The Pillow represents a major theme in her history.

Participant #8 studied with José Limón, first at the Juilliard School, and
then became a member of his company for a period of 21 years. Her work with
the Limón technique and repertory continues today, as she teaches students this
style of dance and stages various works from the Limón Company's extensive
repertory. This professional work became a theme in her life, as did her
profession as a teacher. Another aspect of her professional work involves teaching

the Alexander Technique, and then employing this technique to work with private clients.

Participant #8 believes that her work in the Alexander technique has represented the extent of her psychotherapeutic experience. However, she believes that this has had a major impact upon her life and her teaching. This appears to be another important theme in her life.

Finally, she never studied psychology in school, and has done little reading in this field, with the exception of popularized versions of Gestalt and transpersonal psychology. She seemed interested in the names of the four founders of humanistic psychology, remarked that she was taking down their names to read when "she had the time." However, she was clear throughout the course of this interview that she was "not of the [written] word," and her responses indicate that.

Interview #9 —January 9, 2001. Research Participant #9 was 75 years old at the time of the interview, and still traveling, choreographing new works, and teaching his choreography to new companies. He had been overseas working at the time of my original letter and scheduled an appointment with me upon his return. He was interviewed in his apartment overlooking the East River, which is filled with sunlight, fresh flowers, beautifully bound books, original artwork, and many pieces of ancient sculpture (Hittite, Etruscan, etc.).

He was raised in Pittsburgh, known as "the holy city...because there was a church on every corner" [Participant #9, p.9]. He stated that he

> ...came into dance late. Because I grew up in Pittsburgh, I actually didn't know a thing like dancing existed....I thought I was going to be a writer. My grandmother was a newspaper editor and writer...I had never seen any dance until I was about 16. American Ballet Theatre had come....And I was very close to my English teacher....She was an ardent ballet fan [and] was studying dance....And out of the blue, she said, "Would you like to do this?" [Work as an extra for the Ballet Theatre performances in

Pittsburgh]....

My first vision of dance was being on stage with Ballet Theatre...I saw Antony Tudor's *Romeo and Juliet,* and that just was extraordinary to me; that they could so deeply express something without words....I knew I would love to be part of that. But it was wartime, and I went ahead with my education. [Participant #9, pp.1-2].

He enlisted in the Navy, taking pre-med courses to become a Navy doctor. But he also came to New York City whenever he had liberty and began to study ballet. After World War II, he gave up his plans to become a doctor and returned to New York to continue his study of dance. This action left him without any parental support.

One evening, with 25 cents in his pocket, he sought to borrow some money from a friend who was attending an audition for Jerome Robbins' next show. Robbins saw him, invited him to audition as well, and gave him a contract on the spot. Participant #9 danced as a sailor in *On The Town* in 1946.

Robbins also sent him to study dance with Helen Platova, and he "loved her for all of her deep Russianness, and Russian soul" [Participant #9, p. 3]. Other dancers at Platova's studio spoke to him about another

...wonderful woman...who is working with classical dancers and who is explaining the basis of movement, where movement comes from. And she has an extraordinary technique, a modern pioneer...Hanya Holm. [Hanya Holm had opened the Mary Wigman School of dance in the United States].

I fell in love with Hanya immediately, and became...very, very close to her....I studied with her, learned her technique. Hanya gave me an enormous understanding of movement. She had a very analytical mind.

Especially she [Hanya] freed me in a wonderful way in those improvisational classes. I was usually a kind of shy person. But given the right situation and provocation, then I could actually release, and become quite creative and wild. [Participant #9, pp.4-5]

During this time in his life, Participant #9 finished his studies at New York University, receiving a BS degree. He first encountered Martha Graham at New York University, while demonstrating the dance technique of Hanya Holm. Graham invited him to join her dance company immediately. His loyalty to Holm would not permit him to do this, but he did begin to study with Graham at this time.

So I was working with Hanya. I was also studying with Martha, which Hanya did not know. And I continued my classical training at the same time...was very much an air dancer. I loved to fly in the air....I did develop a big elevation. I loved all of that speed, danger with classical. And I studied with [Antony] Tudor, and [Margaret] Craske at the Met [the old Metropolitan Opera House]. And also with the School of American Ballet....So, it was an amazing, amazing time. [Participant #9, pp.6-7]

He spoke at some length about the differences between the dance techniques of Martha Graham and Hanya Holm. He compared the "gravity based, very deep, and very pelvic style " [Participant #9, p.7] of the early Martha Graham work, with the

...lyricism of Hanya...a feeling of breath...of circle, a very circular technique....And we did many, many exercises which came out of [Hanya's] studies in Germany with [Mary] Wigman and [Rudolf] Laban....That tied me into the classical, as taught by Margaret Craske. [Participant #9, pp.8-9]

When asked who were his most important teachers, Participant #9 listed Hanya Holm first, then Antony Tudor and Margaret Craske. This participant appeared in several Broadway shows that had been choreographed by Hanya Holm. He was also a member of Martha Graham's dance company from 1957 to 1959. He has danced with the following companies: Pearl Lang, Doris Humphrey, Charles Weidman, Pauline Koner, José Limón, John Butler, and he joined the American Ballet Theatre as well as Jerome Robbins' Ballets USA (Long, 1998, p.766). It is clear that Research Participant #9 had a range and diversity of talent that was unique. It was written about him:

> [His] career has been unusually diverse. An appealing and passionate dancer, he was one of the first soloists to work in the various areas of the dance world. He holds a unique place in dance history, being one of the first choreographers to try to blend modern dance with classical ballet. Both as a choreographer and a dancer, he worked in these two areas, and it was his synthesis of these dance forms that characterized his choreographic work. (Long, 1998, p.769)

In 1961, Research Participant #9 began to turn down offers to perform, and devoted himself to becoming a choreographer. His many ballets have become as famous as his dancing.

In 1950, Participant #9 first went to Jacob's Pillow to perform in a piece for Antony Tudor's company. In fact, he stated that "I kept coming up to The Pillow under various guises as a performer. I finally came up with my own company," [Research Participant #9, pp.19-20]. He described Jacob's Pillow in the 1950s.

> It was sort of like a summer camp. A wonderful old log theater, a wooden theater and a very long collection of buildings attached to it, one of which

would be the studio. And the old farmhouse, which was where one ate marvelous meals. There was the old dining room, at which, if Shawn liked you, or you were a special person, you were invited to come sit at this table. Which I got to sit at, I guess because I came up as a performer....I loved it. I mean, to get out of New York City in the summer, and be in those beautiful mountains, and have an enormous amount of freedom. I was able to get one of the original cabins [these were built in the 1930s by the original group of Men Dancers]. [Participant #9, pp.17-18]

Participant #9's relationship with Ted Shawn was marked by a series of ups and downs over the years in which they worked together. He related,

He was a strange person. You sensed immediately an enormous ego. He wanted you to call him "Papa Shawn," very much a founding father....He gave me his book, *Every Little Movement Has a Meaning All its Own* (1963), and inscribed it to me. He liked me very much as a performer....I liked the atmosphere of The Pillow....I didn't find it restrictive.

Eventually I went back when I started to choreograph. When I did my first program...one of the works I had done was a Japanese Noh play, and a beautiful set and costumes by Willa Kim....And I had commissioned a score by a young composer. Shawn wanted that work at The Pillow very much....I said: "This was a commissioned score and I had live music"....And he [Ted Shawn] said: "Well, I really want you to bring that....I will give you the money to have that score recorded." Which was a tremendous gift. [Participant #9, pp.17-19]

Four years later, when Participant #9 used the music of the contemporary composer, Messiaen, for his ballet, *Chronochromie,* Ted Shawn hated the music. He took the time to send this choreographer a negative review from a Lee, Massachusetts newspaper. Shawn triple underlined every negative phrase and concluded: "You see what I mean? You're going to ruin your career!" [Participant #9, p.20].

Participant #9 subsequently returned to Jacob's Pillow with several different companies to present his choreography. On one of these occasions, he explored areas abound The Pillow. He discovered the very large farm next to The Pillow, run by Mother Derby. "She was a very down to earth, extraordinary person...I absolutely loved her. Mother Derby was a real antidote to Papa Shawn. She was so individual, immediate, open and frank" [Participant #9, p.23].

When I began to inquire about psychology, this participant became quite expansive. His discussion covered such topics as religion, mythology, his fascination with archeology, and the psychotherapeutic nature (for him) of travel. He began this discussion:

> I think I've always been interested in psychology. And I've certainly from the early age been aware of Freud and very interested in his concepts; especially about the unconscious and the sexual nature of mankind. And this deep well of experience we have, which is down in the subconscious. I was very interested in reading anything about the creative experience, the creative urge, and about the structure of the brain, the animal brain. [Participant #9, p.27]

He balanced these comments with a discussion of his deeply religious family background and mentioned that his grandfather had been a minister. He mentioned the baptism and immersion ceremonies he had undergone at age 12 or 13. And he reflected,

> And somehow in the heart of it all, I felt a pagan. ...So there was always this conflict of being, looking like a well brought up young adolescent Christian, and in my heart, being a total wild pagan....So I read any psychology that came about....I feel more a Jungian than a Freudian.

[Participant #9, pp.28-29]

He stated that he loved mythology, stating, "You see all of my family gods over there....Etruscan" [Participant #9, p.30]. He pointed to a glass enclosed cabinet filled with ancient Etruscan sculptures, which he discussed with me at some length after the interview had concluded. He stated that Jung had expanded his sphere of thinking, just as his pre-medical education had done. And when he returned to Pittsburgh,

> And full of this new exploration, I went back to the Victorian house, my grandmother's house that I grew up in....And we had a fireplace in the living room, and it had a fireback made of metal....On the back it said, "Man is not a monkey." And I remember having such violent arguments from my grandmother....Anyway, Jung's, *Man and Symbol* was a great book. [Participant #9, pp.30-31]

This participant believed that his exposure to the work of Carl Jung had helped him in his professional work, "because choreography is not just an intellectual act....You have to touch deeper centers to create. It sure helps to have a lot of experience," [Participant #9, p.32].

Participant #9 was unable to recollect reading any of the neo-Freudians, but he appeared to be familiar with the work of Rollo May. It was May's material on mythology that resonated for him, specifically May's connection to Joseph Campbell. Campbell's *The Hero With a Thousand Faces* (1949) was particularly important to this participant, providing him with new ideas for such ballets as *Rite of Spring* and *Mythical Hunters.*

He digressed then to discuss his many experiences in Israel, where he had first gone as a choreographer for Batsheva (a dance company created by Bethsabee Rothschild that featured Martha Graham and her work). He recalled two "religious experiences" that he'd had while in Jerusalem, when he was later invited to return by the Israeli government. He had gone to stay at the American Colony Hotel, which is in East Jerusalem, near the Damascus Gate (into the Old City). He had selected that hotel because he had, "...the journal of my great-grandfather who was a missionary, staying at the American Colony Hotel in 1850....It's built around the central courtyard. It was a real religious experience for me" [Participant #9, p.37].

Another significant "religious experience" for this participant occurred when he had been on The Temple Mount and had gone inside the adjoining mosque itself. The exquisite beauty of the "jewel light that was coming down, and these extraordinary Oriental carpets" [Participant #9, p.37] represented another significant experience for him.

When asked whether he'd had any psychotherapeutic experiences, he laughed and responded, "I think every trip I've taken is a psychotherapeutic experience. I have this fascination for making a journey" [Participant #9, p.38]. He continued to discuss his travels, which carried him all over the world, and search for his roots. He spoke of his reverence for Etruscan places, and his experience upon arriving at one of them for the first time.

> It was not strange. It was all familiar to me. I had come into this place and I was in touch with everything....I was at a place where I belonged....I had been there in a previous lifetime....I belonged there. It was not a strange place....My pagan soul was at home. [Participant #9, pp.39-40]

He also described his use of the *I Ching* (*The Book of Changes*). He has often thrown the *I Ching* in times of doubt, or on the eve of a momentous decision. He stated that he has one important guideline for himself:

> You accept as a dancer that life is a journey and that a career can be brief. That you have to learn to be without fear, to be in constant movement...Not to think that security is a fixed place, because it's not.

[Participant #9, p.42]

It is remarkable that the previous four pages of discussion were evoked by questions about the field of psychology. The expansiveness and range of topics covered makes one recall the words of Abraham Maslow about what psychology should be:

Psychology ought to become more positive and less negative. It should have higher ceilings, and not be afraid of the loftier possibilities of the human being....The meaning of therapy should be expanded to include all the growth-fostering techniques, particularly educational ones, and most particularly creative education in art, in play, and all forms of expression that encourage creativeness, spontaneity, courage and integration. (Maslow, 1957, pp.27-29)

The major themes for Participant #9 began with his many dance teachers. He felt that the most important one was Hanya Holm, because she explained the basis of movement from an anatomical standpoint that his pre-medical training could appreciate. He repeatedly cited Martha Graham, Antony Tudor, and Margaret Craske for being highly significant in his training. Other research participants in this study have listed Craske and Tudor. However, this interviewee is the only one who consciously integrated both the classical techniques and the modern in his dancing and into his choreography.

The Jacob's Pillow Dance Festival played a significant role in Participant #9's performance career: Ted Shawn had liked him and had supported him as a performer and as a choreographer as well. Shawn was generous to him in many instances but also did not hesitate to reprimand him when he employed modern music. The records of Jacob's Pillow reveal that Participant #9 appeared at The Pillow many times, first dancing with different companies and then presenting his own choreography. This participant thoroughly enjoyed the environment of The

Pillow, its natural beauty, and its historical background. He explored the entire area, acquainting himself with The Pillow's neighbors as well.

The theme of psychology provoked an interesting response from this participant. In response to his traditional Christian upbringing, he had read all the psychology he could find, at an early age. He felt that he was more of a Jungian than a Freudian. His only knowledge of the humanistic psychologists was a connection he made between Rollo May's writing about myths and the work of Joseph Campbell. The very subject of psychology aroused an extended conversation about the interviewee's search for his roots, his ancient family gods, and his many transformational experiences while traveling through the world. Although he has never been in psychotherapy, he was clear that he thought that each of his trips had offered him a psychotherapeutic experience.

Interview #10—January 11, 2001. Research participant #10 was 70 years old in 2001; she is the only one of the 70-year-old interviewees who is still dancing as well as choreographing. In 1999, *Dance Magazine* celebrated her 50-year career in dance, acknowledging her outstanding work as a dancer, choreographer, director, actress, teacher, coach and mentor (Tracy, 1999, p.37).

In December 2000, the Alvin Ailey American Dance Theatre presented her newest choreographic piece, *Sweet Bitter Love.* The reviewer for *The New York Times* stated

> They don't make love duets like this anymore. Or rather, it takes a dancer, actor and choreographer of [interview participant's] gifts and experience to create a bare-bones image onstage and fill it with unabashed emotion. (Kisselgoff, 2000)

This participant grew up in East Los Angeles. She began to study dance when she was 14, following in the footsteps of her cousin, Janet Collins, who became the first black dancer to perform in the Metropolitan Opera Ballet (Tracy, 1999, p.37). This interviewee's Creole background combines French, African, and

German ancestry.

Participant #10 was a student of Lester Horton and Bella Lewitzky. At the Horton School she studied music, painting, sculpture, lighting, scenery, acting, ballet, modern, and ethnic dance (Tracy, 1999, p.37). She cited Horton and Lewitzky as her most important modern dance teachers, and Carmelita Maracci as her primary ballet teacher. After Participant #10 graduated from high school, she attended Los Angeles City College. She has few memories of the classes she took at college, since by that time

> I was at Lester's [Horton]. I left home at 6:30 in the morning, to go to school....Then I would go to Lester's, all day, all night And I've never been so tired in my life....Because at that time I was performing, and I was taking classes, and I was maybe teaching children. And it was 7 days a week. [Participant #10, pp.22-23]

She added that once she moved to New York, she studied with Margaret Craske, Hector Zaraspe, and Alfredo Corvino. She first traveled across the country with the Lester Horton Dance Theater in 1950 to perform at the 92nd Street YM-YWHA in New York City. This particular dance company was unique in the 1950s, because it was

> The first racially integrated company in the United States, including black, Mexican-American, Japanese, and white dancers before any other company. His [Lester Horton's] influence has been exercised [and promulgated] through his talented company members and pupils, among whom are Alvin Ailey, Janet Collins, [Participant #10], Bella Lewitzky, Joyce Trisler, and James Truitte. (McDonagh, 1976, p.82)

Despite the success of the Lester Horton Dance Theater and the personal success of this research participant, she did face the racial discrimination that was a part of the dance world in the 1950s and 1960s:

> She was not allowed to perform with Glen Tetley on *The Ed Sullivan Show* because a white man could not partner a black woman on TV. Instead she danced with Ailey partner, Clive Thompson. "We are not going to fly out of orbit if we create a golden race," she said recently...."I know it makes people very nervous, but loosen up, it's the twenty-first century." (Tracy, 1999, p.37)

Participant #10 moved to New York City in 1953, after the death of Lester Horton. She began to perform with an outstanding group of choreographers, including Alvin Ailey, John Butler, Geoffrey Holder (whom she married in 1955), Donald McKayle, and Glen Tetley.

When she was asked about the Jacob's Pillow Dance Festival, she stated casually, that, "because a lot of people were connected to it, it became home, second home as far as performing. So I've been up there since '53,'54.... So, I've just been a mainstay there," [Participant #10, p.7]. In fact, the interviewee performed at the Jacob's Pillow Dance Festival a total of 14 times over the years, which is a record number (Owen, 1997a, pp.46-50).

She reflected upon her times at The Pillow:

> It was a wonderful experience. I just liked being around Shawn because he had so many tales to tell. And then, when I met Miss Ruth...of course that was really a special treat....Oh, we had a wonderful time, I just thought they were the best people. Because those people...were doing things, I mean, going all over the place, other countries. They were really breaking ground. Extraordinary people. And the tales they had to tell are so marvelous....That's what I loved. I liked listening to them, because they were so funny. And you realized it was hard work. [Participant #10, p.8]

Later in this interview, the participant stated, "It was a nice place to work on things. I don't know, it's just that all those spirits are there" [Participant #10, p.12]. When questioned about what she had meant about the spirits, she responded

> Miss Ruth is there, and then Shawn is there. Of course, I don't know if they'd approve of all that jazz....Sometimes I think I can see their spirits going, "Oh my God"...what did they say, "You're fouling the temple" or something like that....I think it's such a rich, beautiful place....Because it has the feeling of the old and then it has the feeling of the new....There's nothing lost....You still have the feeling that it's still the same place. [Participant #10, pp.14-15]

Participant #10 told a remarkable story about her unique relationship to Ted Shawn.

> I know that when he was ill...he said "Come here, sit on my knee," and I sat down. "Yes, Papa." He said, "Would you do something for me? Would you dance at my funeral? I want you to do *The Whole World in His Hands.*" He loved the *Come Sunday* that I did, [from] *The Odetta Suite.* He loved that piece. And I thought about it and I said, "I certainly will." And I forgot about it.
>
> Then Shawn passed away. And I thought, I'm not going to go running around saying Shawn wanted me to dance....So I didn't say anything. Low and behold, Walter Terry called me....He said, "I'm having a little ceremony at The Pillow, and Shawn always liked that piece. Would you do that?"
>
> You see Shawn had told him to do that....So I went up. You see, I believe in stuff like that. I didn't have to say anything. Shawn asked me, I said "yes," and he saw to it that it happened.
>
> So I was the sermon. They'd had a few little things to say, but I

was the sermon. And that one of the greatest compliments I think I have ever gotten in my career. [Participant #10, pp.15-16]

Participant #10 continued to muse about another link she had with Jacob's Pillow.

Miss Ruth was kind to me, too. And after a while I started to feel like Miss Ruth when I was up there as I got older....I did do her *Incense*....It's such a lovely little piece, a tiny little piece. But it's not that easy....Of course nobody could move her arms like Miss Ruth....Her arms were full and round. So she was not angles.... Because it [*Incense*] can easily look corny....You have to believe that you're really in a temple and that the smoke, the fingers follow the smoke up to the gods. Because they [Miss Ruth and Shawn] were always into that, the gods. They were mentally on another plane....It was really like an invocation. Everything was so quiet. And then it was really wonderful because there's the picture of Shawn on one side and Miss Ruth on the other [of the stage]. [Participant #10, pp.15-18]

The research participant mentioned that when she has returned to The Pillow in recent years, she has been surprised at how it has remained unchanged. She acknowledged that there is now a new studio, and reflected

The place is wonderful. But it's all in the flavor of what the original designs were....But it's warm and it's beautiful, and the nice little outdoor theater for the kids [Inside Out], the experimental, and it's lovely....A lot of nice things there. [Participant #10, pp.21-22]

It became clear during this interview that this research participant had many positive recollections of her many times in residence at The Pillow. She summarized firmly, "Oh, it's a magical place" [Participant #10, p.20].

When the interview moved into the area of psychology, the participant stated clearly, "I've never been connected to it" [Participant #10, p.22]. However, she recalled that she had gone to see a psychologist once, and

> He sat there, not saying anything....He was staring at me and I thought...I'd rather have a good friend...or go talk to a tree. I don't know, go to church and sit there and meditate, or something, or figure it out myself....Maybe I never had the right person. [Participant #10, pp.22-24]

She then began to discuss her 9 years with the Yale Repertory Theater. She had been invited there to teach the actors how to move. Soon she was choreographing the plays and performing in them as well. She recalled that she

> ...was with a lot of psychiatrists up there....I would just sit and listen to them. And I gleaned a bit of information. Or I would listen to people...psychoanalyzing other people. You do pick up some information that way....That's about the extent of my psychiatry thing, which is listening to people and observing. [Participant #10, pp.24-25]

She mentioned that she had met Anna Freud, Erik Erikson, and Seymour Lustman when they visited Yale.

Participant #10 continued to reflect upon her time at the Yale Repertory Theater, illuminating how she had synthesized her learning experiences there. She discussed how she had employed psychology as a dancer and as a choreographer.

> And it gave me an extra boost in my dancing really, as far as choreography and observation. Because after being there, around the actors, and their ways of working and observing, I would go back to dance, and I said, "This is not logical"....I'd just question a lot of things....When you're around people who delve into emotions and

personalities because [you realize] that's what their job is, observing people. [Participant #10, pp.25-26]

When this interviewer attempted to have the participant clarify this, she told an elaborate story of her reconstruction of Anna Pavlova's ballet, *Glow, Little Glow Worm,* for the Yale Repertory's production of *The Banquet Years.*

But it was a story and we really told a story...When we worked on it, as long as we kept with the story, our steps came....When we started making up steps, we'd lose it....So I learned something out of that, so that the choreography came out of...whatever you're doing going through or whatever your experience is...If you're going to do a dramatic piece, you have to have something underneath it. At least that's my feeling. [Participant #10, pp.28-29]

She rather modestly summarized what she had learned:

Because at Yale I was working not only with actors, I was working with a top director and playwrights....You listen to them break things down, where you have to have something, some understanding of something....I just kept my mouth shut and ears opened. And so I can draw on certain things and be a little more courageous in my choices. [Participant #10, pp.30-31]

And then, discussing her latest piece of choreography, she demonstrated how she had integrated what she learned at Yale. She had told her dancers,

This is our play....And it was really about the people. We work on the people....But their interpretation, they each had, like each person that does *Hamlet* has a different interpretation....The words are the same but the interpretation, it's open to interpretation....And I will make them work....Each person, you have your story. I'm not telling you mine, you do your work. I know why I do this. [Participant #10, p.32]

This interviewee had incorporated the psychologically oriented work of the Yale Repertory Theater into her own approach to dance and choreography. Although she maintained that she knew nothing about psychology, she had in fact absorbed this orientation, employing it to enhance her own work.

In summary, Participant #10 is remarkable in many ways. At the age of 70, she is not only teaching and choreographing, she is still dancing professionally. As a woman of color, she has had to overcome the racial barriers and prejudices of the dance world. She has bridged this gap, performing in the multiracial companies of Lester Horton and Alvin Ailey, and in the primarily white American Ballet Theatre, and she has choreographed for the predominantly black Dance Theater of Harlem (Ruggiero, 1998, p.188).

She was employed as a dancer to instruct the actors at the Yale Repertory Theater in movement skills. However, her role evolved as she choreographed plays and began to act with the company. She starred in many productions during her 9-year stay in New Haven.

Participant #10 acknowledged Lester Horton and Bella Lewitzky as her primary modern dance teachers. Carmelita Maracci was her first ballet teacher in Los Angeles, and Margaret Craske, Hector Zaraspe, and Alfredo Corvino were her ballet teachers in New York City.

Her connection to the Jacob's Pillow Dance Festival is extensive; in fact, she has performed there on more occasions than any other dancer surveyed. She modestly claimed that it was because she danced with so many companies that had performed at The Pillow. The reality is that this participant established herself as an outstanding dancer, willing and able to handle any of the many challenges placed before her.

Participant #10 also developed strong personal and professional ties to Ted

Shawn and Ruth St. Denis. She was invited by Shawn to perform at his funeral and was permitted to present one of Miss Ruth's most famous dances at one of The Pillow's Gala Performances [these Galas open each summer season]. She stated that she had felt complimented and honored in each case. She believed that the spirits of Shawn and St. Denis evoked the occurrence of events and she was very grateful for each of these opportunities.

Participant #10 stated that she had no background in psychology, and had never done any reading in this field. Her 9 years working with the Yale Repertory Theater allowed her to observe directors, playwrights, and actors psychoanalyzing various roles in rehearsals. She modestly stated, several times, that she had just kept her mouth shut, listened, and observed.

She then discussed her incorporation of this approach into her choreography. She stressed her conviction that each movement must have a meaning and some relevance to the character in the ballet. She stated that her experiences at Yale had increased her options, and had given her more courage in her choreographic choices.

Summary of the Research Interviews

These interviews are remarkable in many ways. I sent out 19 letters to famous American dancers and 10 of them agreed to become participants in this research. There were 5 men and 5 women, and their ages place them in different eras. There was one participant who was 84 at the time of the interview, but has since had a birthday. The next oldest was 85 years old in November 2001. Four participants were in their 70s; two were 75, one is 72, and one of them celebrated a 70th birthday in 2001. Three of the participants were in their 60s, and the youngest was in his mid-50s. One of the outstanding characteristics of this group of modern dancers, like their predecessors (Shaw, St. Denis, Wigman, Graham, and Holm), is that they do not retire from their chosen profession, electing to work until late in their lives. Additionally, this breadth in ages permits exploration of the research questions over four decades.

The differences in educational background are striking: only one of the women graduated from college, and all of the men are college graduates, and Participant #4 has a Masters degree as well. An initial speculation might be that the women started dancing earlier than the men did in the study. Several of the men began to study dance after their time in the military during World War II (Participants #5, #6, #9). Participant #3 began his dance training while at college.

However, this idea doesn't prove accurate. Participant #7 began her dance training at age six, and is the only woman to have graduated from college. Among the men, Participant #4 reported that his dance education began in grade school, and he completed both Bachelor's and Master's degrees. Participant #8 spent 2 years at The Julliard School, and after retiring from her 21 years of performing with the José Limón company, took a 3- year course in the Alexander Technique. She is the only one of the research participants who returned to the classroom when she stopped dancing. She also began her dance training at the age of 6.

Therefore, the age at which the research participants began their dance training does not explain why so few of the women continued their education into college. My assumption would be that most of these women were already deeply involved in their professional work at a very early age. This was certainly true of Participants #1, 2, 7, and 10. Only Participant #7 was able to attend Mills College and combine both her dance and academic interests. Perhaps the answer is revealed by Participant #10, who described the incredible demands placed upon her when she was dancing professionally and taking college courses.

When we examine the selected list of teachers chosen by the dancers as their most important teachers, several interesting connections and similarities are revealed. Many of the participants studied with Martha Graham (#1, #4, #5, #9, #10), but only participants #1 and #9 thought that she had profoundly influenced their professional work. Participants #4 and #5 had been offered scholarships by Martha Graham, but they had not wanted to confine their dancing to the Graham technique. Participant #10 had felt more physically comfortable with the Lester Horton technique.

Hanya Holm was cited by 4 of the interviewees as one of their most important dance teachers (Participants #1, #4, #6, and #9). We must note that Alvin Nikolais was a student of Hanya Holm, and he was listed as the most important dance teacher for Participants #2 and #6. Holm's contributions to growth and development of modern dance in American are discussed in the literature review and are illustrated here by the acknowledgment of the dancers in this study.

Many of the dancers studied ballet in addition to modern dance. Margaret Craske taught 3 of the participants (#8, #9, and #10), and Antony Tudor was mentioned by participants #8 and #9. Both of these ballet teachers taught at Jacob's Pillow, in addition to teaching in New York City.

All of the dancers in this study are connected in some way to the Jacob's Pillow Dance Festival. This was one of the criteria for their inclusion in this study. There were several ways in which these participants established their linkage to this dance festival. All of them have danced at The Pillow at least once.

Participant #1 performed with Ted Shawn and Ruth St. Denis in their Sacred Dance Guild, which was a preseason event. When her company was performing at The Pillow in 1957, she taught at the school and returned as a teacher in 1973. In 2001, 44 years later, she returned to Jacob's Pillow once again and performed in *From The Horse's Mouth.*

Participant #2 performed at Jacob's Pillow twice, with the Murray Louis dance company.

Participant #3 performed at The Pillow 6 times during the 1970s and 1980s. In 1990, he and his company were asked to re-create The Men Dancers in honor of the 100th anniversary of Ted Shawn's birth. They were in residence at Jacob's Pillow for extended periods of time in 1991, and again in 1992, in order to accomplish this goal.

Participant #4 stated that he had danced at The Pillow several times with various dance companies. He brought his own dance company up to Jacob's Pillow only once, in 1968.

Participant #5 performed at Jacob's Pillow 3 times: in 1942, with Helen Tamiris; in 1958, he performed the solos for which he is renowned; and in the 1990s, he joined Danny Buraczeski in performance. He is the only one of the research participants who danced at The Pillow over a 50-year time span. One of the three books he wrote is appropriately titled *How to Dance Forever*.

Participant #6 performed at Jacob's Pillow many times. He appeared with his own company 7 times and as the director of Nikolais and Murray Louis Dance in 1996.

Participant #7 first performed at Jacob's Pillow in 1980, and has returned a total of 7 times since then. Her last performance at The Pillow was in 1999. She also teaches composition classes when she is at The Pillow.

Participant #8 first came to Jacob's Pillow as a student, and returned for 3 summers. She was in one of the first student groups to be allowed to perform at The Pillow. She returned later, as a member of the José Limón Dance Company in 1974. This participant was also on the faculty at The Pillow, and has returned to teach Master classes there.

Participant #9 performed at Jacob's Pillow dance festival 5 times with various companies with whom he danced. He brought his own dance company there twice and premiered one of his most famous pieces of choreography, *Chronochomie*, at Jacob's Pillow in 1966.

Participant #10 performed at Jacob's Pillow a total of 14 times, more than any of the other research participants. She was able to achieve this because she danced with many companies (Alvin Ailey, Geoffrey Holder, Lester Horton Dance Theatre, Donald McKayle, and Glen Tetley & Company). She also brought her own dance company, she danced several programs of duets, and appeared as a solo dancer several times. This participant was invited to perform a solo at Ted Shawn's memorial service in 1972. While in residence at The Pillow, she taught the Lester Horton technique and stagecraft classes.

The 10 research participants were in agreement on one subject only: they all responded to the physical beauty of the site of the Jacob's Pillow Dance

Festival. Participant #1 recalled the natural beauty of the woods, in which she had walked many times. She also discussed the historical importance of the creation of the Men Dancers, who had constructed many of the original buildings found at The Pillow today.

Participant #2 felt that the site had been lovely. Participant #3 enjoyed the country setting and he believed that Pilobolus had found the Pillow to be a most congenial environment for their work. He noted that the Pilobolus company had also chosen to have their studios outside of New York City.

Participant #4 said that he had enjoyed the beauty of Jacob's Pillow. Participant #5 stated that his times at The Pillow had been lovely experiences. He recalled that it was a focused environment, where he felt that everyone was on his side. He knew that this type of environment was a very hard thing to find in the United States.

Participant #6 stated that he had loved The Pillow because he enjoyed the ambiance. He discussed his times staying at High Folly (a nearby guesthouse), which had allowed him to get to know the other dancers who had been on the program with him. He had also taken the time to investigate the history of Jacob's Pillow.

Participant #7 spoke about how much she had enjoyed getting out of the city, reflecting that she really was a country girl. She also recalled the fine vegetarian food that was served at The Pillow. Participant #8 was equally delighted with The Pillow's natural environment, for similar reasons. She stated that her spiritual connections had always been through nature. She remembered Jacob's Pillow as a perfect place for the dancer because "you eat, sleep, drink, and breathe dance."

Participant #9 recalled that Jacob's Pillow was like a summer camp, and that " I loved...to be out of New York City, and in those beautiful mountains, and [to] have an enormous amount of freedom." This participant also went out of his way to stay in one of the original houses built by the Men Dancers.

Participant #10 agreed with the other 9 interviewees, but she had a different interpretation of what made Jacob's Pillow so special for her. She remembered that The Pillow had been a wonderful place to work on things because "the spirits of Miss Ruth and Papa Shawn are there. It's a rich and beautiful place, combining the old and the new. It's a magical place."

Almost all of the research participants discussed their relationship with and their connections to Ruth St. Denis and Ted Shawn. This was striking because the research protocol does not contain this specific question. However, in qualitative research, material tends to arise from the data and should be addressed. Because most of the interviewees dealt with this matter, their reflections are included in this summary.

Participant #1 was quite firm in her belief that both Ted Shawn and Ruth St. Denis were historically important. She stated that their (Denishawn) contribution had been underestimated, and she recalled that Martha Graham had received her original dance training from a Denishawn school. She also stressed the importance of the Men Dancers, the first all male American dance company, which toured throughout the United States.

Participant #2 remembered meeting Ted Shawn for the first time, reflecting that "he was quite wonderful." He had welcomed the company to The Pillow, had explained the "Holy ground that we were rehearsing on," and made "reference to the studio where so many people have rehearsed. And he made references to the photographs. And then he left" [Participant #2, p.5]. She also recalled having seeing Ruth St. Denis perform *White Jade* at the Henry Street Settlement Playhouse when the participant was an adolescent. When the curtain opened, Miss Ruth was sitting on a pedestal, "looking so ravishing. We were awestruck....And the kids said, 'It's God, it's God'....That's the transformation....it said everything about a woman's transcendancy. It said everything about theater. And it was wonderful...Her powers were extraordinary" [Participant #2, pp.6-8].

Participant #3 had performed at Jacob's Pillow for the first time after Ted Shawn's death in 1972. Nonetheless, he felt a link to Shawn through his choreography. When Pilobolus was working on the re-creation of the Men Dancers (in 1990), Participant #3 felt that his company's work bore a connection to Shawn's early choreography. He stated that Pilobolus felt that "it was a harmonious fit. The piece...was *Kinetic Molpai.* And I thought it was a very inventive, modern piece, I thought it was very freshly conceived" [Participant #3, p.8].

Participant #4 felt that he had not been influenced by Jacob's Pillow, but believed that he had been influenced by what Ted Shawn had written, by the pictures of Denishawn performances, and by knowing Barton Mumaw.

Participant #5 recalled dinners at The Pillow, when Ted Shawn and Ruth St. Denis were telling stories about their Denishawn experiences, each one trying to top the other. He also recalled meeting Shawn during World War II, when Shawn had followed Barton Mumaw to his army basic training site. Both Participant #5 and Barton Mumaw shared fond memories of their times together in the Army, and later, when they shared a part in the Broadway show, *Annie Get Your Gun.*

Participant #6 stated that he had gotten to know Ted Shawn very well. He deplored the fact that in the last years of his life, Ted Shawn had been ignored by the public. This interviewee had also spent time observing the school of dance at Jacob's Pillow and had been favorably impressed by its diversity. Shawn had known of Participant #6's success as the director of the school at the Henry Street Settlement Playhouse. Shawn had offered to make Participant #6 the director of the school at Jacob's Pillow. Although this interviewee had refused this offer, he was very proud to have been offered this opportunity.

Participant #7 did not discuss any connections to either Ted Shawn or Ruth St. Denis. There could be two reasons for this. First, she performed at Jacob's Pillow after both Shawn and St. Denis had died. Second, as a post-modernist choreographer, she was focused upon eliminating all of the literary and emotional symbolism that had guided the works of the Denishawn Company. Because this question was not on the protocol, her feelings about these two pioneers of modern dance could not be explored, only assumed. This assumption can be substantiated by the research interview.

Research Participant #8 remembered Ted Shawn with ambivalence. She gave him credit for being a tenacious believer and for having established Jacob's Pillow. She recalled his "curtain warmer" speeches before each performance that were so informative. She also reflected that he had brought an entirely new audience to see dance, the whole range of dance. She then recalled that Shawn had been extremely egotistical and finally, "He was impossible."

Participant #9 also had mixed memories of Ted Shawn. He recalled that Shawn had an enormous ego, and was very much a "founding father—he wanted you to call him 'Papa Shawn'" [Participant #9]. He remembered that Shawn could be very generous, because Shawn had funded the recording of a piece of live music, which allowed his new ballet to be presented at The Pillow. When Participant #9 had brought another new work to The Pillow (which had very contemporary music), Shawn was outraged. Shawn had liked Participant #9 enough to make certain that he was always seated at Shawn's table, a place of honor.

Participant #10 recalled both Ted Shawn and Ruth St. Denis with great fondness. She had been invited by an ailing Shawn to perform one of his favorite dances at his funeral and she had agreed. Subsequently, she was asked to dance at the memorial service for Ted Shawn, and she believed that this was one of the greatest honors that she had ever received. She stated that she had always felt close to Miss Ruth, particularly as she got older. When she invited to perform *Incense,* one of St. Denis' most famous pieces, at a Pillow Gala in 1997, she felt honored once again.

Some might assume that higher education was a prerequisite for any knowledge of psychology. The participants in this study refute this notion, displaying a wide range of interest and knowledge in psychological topics. However, with one exception (#9), none of the participants were familiar with the writings of Rollo May, Abraham Maslow, Carl Rogers, or James Bugental. The neo-Freudians, Karen Horney and Erich Fromm, were more recognizable names to the research participants, as well as Freud and Jung, who were the best known names. The individual responses to the questions about psychology revealed a wide range of interest and knowledge. However, the participants were familiar with the ideas underlying humanistic psychology.

Participant #1 stated that she had read Sigmund Freud, Carl Jung, Karen Horney, Erich Fromm, and Wilhelm Reich. She stressed her interest in Reich's work because of his emphasis upon the body and what the body revealed. Participant #2 said she never read any psychology because it didn't interest her.

Participant #3 stated that he had done extensive reading in psychology while in college, recalling Erik Erikson, B. F. Skinner, Jean Piaget, and R. D. Laing. This participant recognized the name of Rollo May but had read none of his work. Participant #4 had also done extensive reading in psychology during his Masters program. He recalled reading the work of Karen Horney, Erich Fromm, Joseph Moreno (the psychodramatist), and Marian Chace.

Participant #5 had originally planned to be a psychiatrist or a social worker and had done extensive reading in the field of psychology. He said that he had read some of Freud, Horney, and Fromm. He seemed familiar with the work of the behaviorists but volunteered no names. Participant #6 stated that he was totally familiar with the writings of Freud, Jung, Alfred Adler, and William James. He thought that Erich Fromm's books were much too long.

Participant #7 said that she had read Freud at school and was familiar with the writings of Fritz Perls and Laura Perls. She had been at Esalen and became aware of the collaborative work of Fritz Perls and Anna Halprin. Participant #8 stated that she had never taken any psychology courses but had read the work of Fritz Perls, and all of Shirley MacLaine's transpersonally oriented books. It is striking that only these two women in their 60s mentioned the work of either or both of the Perls'.

Participant #9 stated that he had been deeply interested in the theories of Freud, particularly those dealing with human sexuality and the unconscious. Jung had greatly interested this participant because of his focus upon symbolism, mythology, and the collective unconscious. He stated that he had been most influenced by the writings of Jung. Participant #9 knew about Rollo May's work on mythology, and stressed May's alleged connection to Joseph Campbell.

Participant #10 stated that she had never done any reading in psychology and that she had no knowledge of the field. Her subsequent discussion illuminated the fact that, through her extended exposure to the analytically oriented Stanislavski techniques at the Yale Repertory Theater, she had developed a psychological approach to her dancing and her choreography.

To summarize, it appears that the older members of this study (those in their 70s and 80s) were familiar with the work of Freud, Jung, Adler, Reich, Horney, and Fromm. Those participants in their 60s were acquainted with the work of Fritz Perls. The participant in his 50s (#3) reported extensive readings in psychology, but only the writing of a later generation (Erikson, Piaget, Skinner, and Laing). Apparently there is a correlation between the age of the participant and which psychologists they have read. The level of education appears to be less important than the degree of interest in the subject.

Four of the research participants (#1, #6, #8, and #9) reported that they had never been to see a psychologist or a psychotherapist. However, Participant #8 stated that learning the Alexander Technique had been psychotherapeutic for her, and tremendously helpful. Participant #9 stated that every one of his journeys had been a psychotherapeutic experience for him.

Participant #2 had been to see therapists twice and reported that each encounter had changed her life in a significant fashion.

Participant #3 had a variety of experiences with psychotherapists. He had gone into family therapy to support his son's struggle with Attention Deficit Disorder. When problems arose within his closely-knit, collaborative dance company, the whole group had gone into family therapy. The therapist who worked with the Pilobolus company is a renowned family therapist and philosophically a direct descendant of Rollo May, Carl Rogers, Harry Stack

Sullivan, and Erich Fromm.

Participant #4 had a series of psychotherapeutic experiences that mirror the evolution of psychotherapy in the United States. This interviewee first had an in-depth analysis. His next experience with therapy was described as "sitting-up, face-to-face therapy." Finally, he spent several years in group therapy. The therapists with whom he worked also reflected the manner in which the psychotherapeutic process had evolved during the 20th century.

Participant #5 reported two very brief psychotherapeutic experiences. He described the second one as very helpful. He discussed a life-altering incident in which he had literally stood outside of himself, and spoke to another part of himself (his Inner Critic). He had then moved to his typewriter to describe the entire experience. Since that time, Participant #5 has employed writing as a psychotherapeutic tool for himself. This process of separation between the selves, the emergence of an evaluative, or supportive self, and another self emerging as a witness, is typical of a Voice Dialogue session. The participant's use of writing as a therapeutic modality is contemporary as well. *The Creative Journal* by Lucia Capacchione (1987) discusses moving from a Voice Dialogue session into journalling to extend and support the therapeutic process.

Participant #6 reported no formal psychotherapy. He discussed how his personal psychology involved different selves: one part was "the me," and there were other selves such as the dancer and the teacher. He stated that he would always choose in favor of the part that was using the body. He also believed that this embodied self was "Not the ego me," who he characterized as happy go-lucky and who preferred to garden and eat. This participant was completely comfortable with his version of separate subpersonalities. He clearly enjoys conducting his own form of Voice Dialogue sessions, which helps him to arrive at conclusions.

Participant #7 reflected that her years in non-Freudian psychotherapy had been very helpful to her professionally. She reflected that she had needed to invent herself, to write her own story choreographically. Her psychotherapeutic experience had supported this growth. She also reported supportive dialoguing between her different selves, a familiar Voice Dialogue experience.

Participant #8 stated that the Alexander technique had been her whole therapy. She explained that this technique allowed her to make personal changes by changing her thoughts. She stressed the mind/body connection and her belief that the Alexander technique had empowered her in many ways. Her description of an Alexander bodywork session resembled a humanistic psychotherapy session, i.e., the therapist is completely present in the moment and is not trying to fix or to manipulate the client.

Participant #9 stated that every one of his many journeys had been a psychotherapeutic experience for him. He portrayed his travels as supporting his ongoing search for a " psychic home" for his "pagan soul." Several of his journeys took him into places that he felt he had known in a previous lifetime. Although Participant #9 had never seen a psychotherapist, his travels and his use of the *I Ching* had served as replacements for him.

Participant #10 had been to see a psychologist once and had never returned. She stated that she might have been better off talking to a friend or a tree, or trying to meditate.

Finally, each one of the research participants volunteered additional material that which had not been sought on the protocol. This section of the summary permits them to speak once again.

Participant #1 had a strong religious background, which was reflected throughout her career. She choreographed, performed, and taught in a series of religiously oriented programs throughout the 1950s and 1960s. She maintains a strong connection to the various creative arts, which she uses to create a series of images, employed in her teaching and in her choreography.

Participant #2 stated that she was strongly influenced by the visual arts because she believes that the same principles apply to her compositions. She volunteered that she was deeply involved in a mentoring program for young choreographers, which has been sponsored by the Joyce Theater.

Participant #3 stressed the nature of the collaborative creativity in the choreographic output of the Pilobolus Company. This process has been enhanced by the reading and personal experiences of the group members.

Participant #4 spoke at length about how important teaching dance and theater had been in his life. He stressed that this had been both challenging and stimulating to him throughout the years.

Participant #5 stressed the impact of Helen Tamiris' work and how her originality had strongly influenced him and his professional work. He also discussed his evolving ability to sit still at this time in his life. He reiterated how he used writing to help himself through difficult times.

Participant #6 reflected how important his teaching had been to him, particularly when he was teaching the young children at the Henry Street Settlement House.

Participant #7 also discussed the impact of visual arts upon her choreography. She highlighted how important her music and composition teachers had been to the evolution of her strongly original choreography. She also discussed at length the on-going support she had received from the French government for her teaching and her choreography.

Participant #8 was a student (and eventually a teacher) of Labanotation. She was very proud to have received an acknowledgement from Ted Shawn (1963) in his book, *Every Little Movement.* She is currently teaching Limón technique and repertory as well as Alexander Technique.

Participant #9 stressed the impact of his strongly Christian upbringing upon his "pagan soul." He has searched throughout the world to discover his historical roots, and has experienced many religious moments and spiritual revelations on these journeys.

Participant #10 discussed how her work with the Yale Repertory Theater had given her new insights, providing her with many new options for both her dancing and her choreography.

Table 1 is a matrix that summarizes the interviews with the dancers.

Table 1A
Participant Demographics

Participant	Age	Gender	Education	Additional material Volunteered in Interview
1	85	F	High School Graduate	Strong religious background shown in work. Other creative arts help her create imagery in teaching, choreography.
2	63	F	High School Graduate	Very strongly influenced by visual arts. Same principles apply to dance and art. Mentors 3 young choreographers.
3	53	M	B.A., Dartmouth	Need for ongoing group process for collaborative creativity.
4	72	M	B.A., M.A.U., Wisconsin	Worked at psychiatric hospital doing movement therapy during M.A. program. Considers teaching dance, acting very important.
5	85	M	B.S., City College, NY	Validity and important of Helen Tamiris' work. Has voice dialogue-like experiences. Now "learning how to sit still."
6	75	M	B.A., New York University	Teaching the children and running the Henry Street Settlement School very important. Dialogues with his selves.
7	64	F	B.A., Mills College	Impact of visual arts, stressing structures, geometrical *vs.* sequential in work. Music composition training very important. Strong support from French for her work.
8	61	F	2 yrs. Julliard, 3 yrs. Alexander training	Danced with José Limón for 21 years. Labanotation trained. Teaches Limón technique and repertory. Alexander Technique (uses on clients.)
9	75	M	B.S., New York Univ.	Impact of Christian Family upon his "pagan soul;" has searched world for his roots, "Home." Traveling produces religious, transcendent experiences.
10	70	F	High School Graduate	Stressed how the psychological impact of her work at Yale Repertory Theatre taught her new ideas which she integrated into her own dancing and choreography.

Table 1B
Participant Dance Teachers and Connections to Jacob's Pillow

P#	Most Important Dance Teachers	Links to Jacob's Pillow Dance Festival	Personal Responses to Jacob's Pillow Site	Connections to Ted Shawn, Ruth St. Denis
1	Hanya Holm, Martha Graham	Sacred Dance Guild performed 2x, taught 2x more	Loved the beauty of the woods, historical importance of Men Dancers	"Both were historically important. Martha Graham was trained by them."
2	Alwin Nikolais, Merce Cunningham, Zena Rommet, Robert Joffrey, Luigi	Performed 2x w/Murray Dance Co.	"It was lovely but I wasn't invited back." Very political place.	Seeing St. Denis perform, " and her Transformation was a transcendent moment."
3	Took one class at Dartmouth	Performed w/Pilobolus 6x in 199s. In residence 2x for Men Dancers Touring Group	Loved the "country vibe," felt choreographic links to Men Dancers	Did choreography linked to Men Dancers; studied Shawn's choreography
4	Hanya Holm, Marge H'Douber, Louse Klepper, Irene Daley (acting)	Performed 1x w/his own group and w/other groups	Enjoyed the beauty; influenced by Shawn's writings, meeting other dancers	Only felt influenced by Shawn's writings
5	Helen Tamiris, Rae Moses, Anna Sokolow, Mme. A. Ivantzove. Acting: M. Goldina, S. Meisner, Stella Adler	Performed 6x	Lovely experience, very focused. "Everyone's on your side!" Rare to find that support in US	Met Shawn during his Army service w/Barton Mumaw; rivalry between St. Denis, Shawn
6	Alwin Nikolais, Hanya Holm	Performed 7x	Loved it all, "the ambiance, knowing the other dancers." Studied Jacob's Pillow's history	Shawn was historically important; offered the directorship of The Pillow school

Table 1B, Cont'd.
Participant Dance Teachers and Connections to Jacob's Pillow

P#	Most Important Dance Teachers	Links to Jacob's Pillow Dance Festival	Personal Responses to Jacob's Pillow Site	Connections to Ted Shawn, Ruth St. Denis
7	Marian Ajgeage, Louis Horst, Anna Halprin, Bob Dunn, Doris Dennyson	Performed 7x, had dances commissioned by Jacob's Pillow	"Grand to be out of the city; I'm a nature girl."	None
8	Margaret Craske, Ann Hutchinson, José Limón, Antony Tudor, Jean Cébron	Studied 3 summers, 2x w/José Limón. Taught Master Classes in Limón, Alexander techniques	"Jacob's Pillow was the perfect place. My inspiration, spiritual connections are through nature."	Had classes, lectures w/Shawn: "He built a new awareness of the diversity of dance."
9	Hanya Holm, Antony Tudor, Margaret Craske, Helen Platova, Martha Graham	Performed 2x w/own company. Premiers 2 new works. Performed many times in other groups.	Loved to be out of NYC; "Those beautiful mountains, with great freedom to work."	Shawn was "very much a founding father. Always sat at his table." Shawn unhappy about his use of music.
10	Bella Lewitzky, Carmelita Maracci, Margaret Craske, Hector Zaraspe, Alfredo Corvino	Performed 16x w/her own and other companies. Taught Horton Technique, stagecraft	"A rich and beautiful place, Combining old and new. A magical place, because the spirits of Shawn and St. Denis are present."	Very close personal relationship w/Shawn, St. Denis. "Invited by Shawn to dance at his funeral, Which I did."

Table 1C
Participant Connections to Psychology

P#	Knowledge of Psychology (Humanistic, Psychoanalysis)	Psychotherapeutic Experience
1	Read Freud, Jung, W. Rich, K. Horney, E. Fromm, W. Reich	None
2	Never did any reading in field; "not interest."	2x w/psychiatrist. Each time was "life changing."
3	Extensive reading in psychology classes; not of humanistic psychology	Did family therapy in own family. Pilobolus group did family therapy with theoretical descendant of humanist psychologists
4	Reading in M.A. program: E. Fromm, K. Horney, J. Moreno, M. Chace	3x; 1st w/psychoanalyst, 2nd w/student of T. Reik; then was in group therapy
5	Freud, behaviorists, K. Horney, E. Fromm	"A few sessions with Freudian;" 6x at Payne Whitney Clinic in NYC. Now "I handle my own problems" by writing.
6	"Totally familiar with Jung, Freud, Adler, Fromm, William James."	None, but does dialog w/his different selves to find answers to his questions
7	Read Freud in school; Fritz Perls, Laura Perls	Some years in therapy. "Very helpful because I needed to invent myself professionally."
8	No psychology course; read F. Perls, all of Shirley MacLaine	"Alexander technique has been my therapy."
9.	Very influenced by Jung, Freud, Rollo May's work on myths	"Every trip I've taken has been a psychotherapeutic experience."
10.	None (see additional material, Table 1A)	"Saw a psychologist 1x only

Chapter 5

Discussion

I undertook this study because it seemed apparent to me that there were many striking similarities between the evolution of humanistic psychology and the development of modern dance in America. One similarity between the two groups was the manner in which the ideas were passed from generation to generation. Another similarity was that both modern dance and humanistic psychology evolved from a rebellious stance and the wish to exercise increased personal and professional freedom. A third similarity between these two was their increasing response to the world around them and their connections to the zeitgeist of the 20th century. The four humanistic psychologists studied here represent the third generation in their field, as do the 10 dancers who were interviewed.

In psychoanalysis, Sigmund Freud had a group of analysts whom he had personally trained. These analysts included Alfred Adler, Sandor Ferenczi, Carl Jung, and Otto Rank, all of whom became dissenters from Freudian orthodoxy. The theories of Ferenczi and Rank were transmitted through their books and papers to the next generation of analysts, the neo-Freudians. The neo-Freudians included European -born Karen Horney, Erich Fromm, and Frieda Fromm-Reichmann, and the American Clara Thompson and Harry Stack Sullivan.

In earlier studies (Hoffman, 1996a, 1996b; Hoffman, 1997b), I documented how the ideas of the neo-Freudians influenced the four pioneers of humanistic psychology, Abraham Maslow, Rollo May, Carl Rogers, and James Bugental. It was also possible to document the ways in which Ferenczi's innovative theories were transmitted through the neo-Freudians to the humanistic psychologists. Otto Rank, another dissenter from the Freudian school, collaborated with Ferenczi and had an acknowledged impact upon the thinking of Carl Rogers.

I had hoped to discover that there were connections that had been made in previous generations as well as contemporaneously, between the modern dancers and the psychologists. The archival/database literature review illustrated that some dancers in the second generation of modern dancers were familiar with the early writers in psychoanalysis and psychology.

The results of my inquiry are only partially apparent in Table 1, the summary of the research interviews. The archival/database literature review revealed that the evolution of modern dance had little or no impact upon Maslow, May, Rogers, and Bugental. One of my speculations in undertaking this study was that these four psychologists would show some ongoing interest in this subject, because it evolved in a parallel manner to the development of humanistic psychology. The literature review included the topics of dance, dancing, and dance/movement therapy, in addition to an exploration of creativity.

Maslow wrote about dancing within the context of his studies of creativity. He displayed a profound understanding of the improvisational aspects of dancing and psychotherapy. He stressed the need for creativity in teaching methods and emphasized the significance of the creative arts for the self-actualized person.

May emphasized that the arts were always grounded within a cultural context, and that one could not understand any art form outside of its culture. He wrote about folk dance specifically as the reflection of a given culture, because he believed that he had learned about one culture through his participation in folk dancing.

Rogers discussed the use of physical movement during encounter groups as an occurrence that others practiced. He was clear about his personal discomfort in moving within the groups that he led and did not explore this further. Bugental's early discussions about the essential importance of embodiment to the pursuit of authenticity were not pursued in his later work. It was only through my personal communications with Bugental and his wife, that I discovered their great interest in modern dance. Unfortunately, these four notable humanistic psychologists did not discuss the development of modern dance within the scope of their professional writing.

This study has revealed that modern dance has followed a similar evolutionary process and that it has occurred within the same time frame as psychoanalytic innovations. Ted Shawn and Ruth St. Denis ran the Denishawn Company from 1915 through 1930, touring extensively throughout the United States, Europe, and the Orient. They represented the American forms of modern dance. Mary Wigman began her pioneering journey in 1915, developing her version of modern dance in response to the realities of her contemporary German culture. Wigman was one of the leaders of the German Expressionistic Movement, which reflected that culture in dance, art, and music. Although Shawn stated that he had not been impressed by Wigman's innovations he did invite one of her leading students to teach at the Denishawn School, and later at the Jacob's Pillow School of the Dance.

During the 1915-1930 era, many psychoanalytic pioneers separated themselves from Freudian doctrine. They were also travelling through the world, introducing their new theories and ideas. There is little documentation of any connections made between the first generations of modern dancers (Shawn, St. Denis, and Wigman) and the evolving field of psychology.

The next generation of modern dancers is represented in this study by Martha Graham and Hanya Holm. They were both established dancers by the 1930s; they both continued to dance for many years and they both taught and choreographed for the next 60 years. There is documentation of Graham's several connections to the work of Jung, both personally and professionally. Holm demonstrated her familiarity with the evolving field of psychology, contrasting the work of Freud and Jung in her writing. Holm was uniquely aware of the impact of the zeitgeist upon her work and brought this awareness into her dance studio and her choreography. She educated her students in dance history, as well as in anatomy.

Graham and Holm performed the neo-Freudian function within the field of modern dance. The neo-Freudians utilized the theories of many of the psychoanalytic pioneers, adding their own humanizing points of view. It has been said that the neo-Freudians Americanized psychoanalysis. Graham and Holm took the dance forms created by Shawn, St. Denis, and Wigman, and added their own innovations. The modern dances created by Holm and Graham were more basically rooted in the American experience than previous choreographic works.

The pioneers of humanistic psychology represent a third generation, which developed new ways of conceptualizing psychological theory, process, and connections to the world around them. The third generation of modern dancers (those interviewed for this study) reflects the evolution of modern dance into expansive new dimensions. These 10 dancers exhibit great diversity in their dance training, choreographic experiences, and in their familiarity with psychology and the psychotherapeutic process. They all reflect significant connections to the American zeitgeist.

The three generations of dance/movement therapists in this study also reflect historical trends. Marian Chace, the first dance/movement therapist, who began this phase of her career in the 1940s, did not reveal any of the psychological bases of her professional work. Her dance teachers and contemporaries, Shawn and St. Denis, also did not reflect any psychological background or awareness. Chace learned her psychology on the wards of St. Elizabeth's Hospital and in the training sessions provided for the staff there. She continued her studies with Harry Stack Sullivan and Frieda Fromm-Reichmann.

In the second generation of dance/movement therapists, Penny Bernstein Lewis performed the neo-Freudian function. Her work has been both integrative and theoretical. Lewis has written extensively, presenting the ideas of Marian Chace alongside the work of Freud, Adler, Jung, and Fritz Perls.

The third generation of dance/movement therapists is represented in this study by Fran Levy and Ilene Serlin. They are the only dance movement therapists who have systematically acknowledged the work of the humanistic psychologists. In a literature review of dance/movement therapy, Serlin and Levy are also the most consistently reflective of humanistic psychology within the American zeitgeist.

It has been in the third generation in which the most concrete connections have appeared between the psychologists, the dancers and the dance/movement therapists. This linkage has been documented throughout this study. Furthermore, it is this third generation that most embodies the personal and professional freedom that characterized the development of both humanistic psychology and American modern dance. The contemporary dancers and the psychologists continue to evolve, to develop new ideas, and to move in innovative new directions.

The Handbook of Humanistic Psychology (Schneider, Bugental, & Pierson, 2001) documents the many ways in which growth is continuing at this time. Humanistic psychology has become more inclusive of many aspects of contemporary American life. This book reveals an enhanced appreciation of spirituality, a validation for the relevance of the personal myth, an acknowledgement of body/mind medicine, and a respectful place for our strivings to preserve our planet (ecology) and live in a peaceful world. Humanistic psychology has also encouraged and legitimized the development of newer forms of qualitative research methodologies, removing psychology from its dependence upon the rules and restrictions of laboratory science.

The third generation of modern dancers interviewed herein has revealed an unwillingness to be bound by any forms at all. Several of them reflect a strong connection to the visual arts and one of them explores space from an architectural viewpoint. Spontaneity and collective creativity support their newest choreographic works. Music has become an option, rather than a necessity, for the newest forms of dance. This third generation reflects an acute awareness of the contemporary world, addressing such issues as spirituality, the challenge of personal illness, and the catastrophic events of September 11th, 2001.

This third generation has provided the most concrete connections between the psychologists, the dancers, and the dance/movement therapists. This group is the most reflective of the evolution of two separate systems of creativity through a shared zeitgeist, that of 20th century American culture.

Limitations and Delimitations

The limitations of this study are several. There were 10 participants and one interviewer, who then became the only analyst of the interview material. There was no cross checking by others of the results for bias, reliability, or accuracy. The interviewer was cognizant of the participants' conscious desire to please, to inform, and to be cooperative. The one exception was Participant #5, who, from time to time, became annoyed with me.

Although I made efforts to insure the anonymity of the participants, this did not appear to limit the results. In fact, most of the interviewees spoke freely, without apparent concern about being identifiable. I attempted to remove all identifiers that were not relevant to the interview process.

The delimitations of the study apply to the original decision-making process. I elected to work with modern dance rather than ballet because modern dance is a continuously evolving field, as is the field of psychology. When I limited the study to dancer/choreographers who had connections to Jacob's Pillow Dance Festival, it narrowed the field of potential interview participants considerably.

Finally, I elected to limit my study to four humanistic pioneers, Maslow, May, Rogers, and Bugental. I made this selection because I think that they have articulated most clearly the ideals of humanistic psychology from its inception and during many of the years of its evolutionary process.

Conclusions

Gilbert (1976), in his dissertation, *Jazz, Rock and Roll, and the Revolution in Psychotherapy,* suggests that the arts (specifically popular music) could forecast shifts in psychology and in the culture itself. My study demonstrates that modern dance has been both predictive and reflective of the cultural soil in which it has been nurtured. The changing mores of the 20th century have permitted modern dancers to embody the increasing liberation of the human body and the shifting of gender roles that has occurred. As the world of psychology has expanded and developed, so has modern dance shifted and changed. The cultural environment has enriched the evolution of modern dance, with the contributions of the psychologists adding to the enhancement. The evolution of modern dance, as discussed in this study, has been reflective of the American zeitgeist, as well as predictive of its changes.

There will be many studies of the trends of the 20th century. Psychology, modern dance, and dance/movement therapy all developed throughout this century. There are times and places in which the three different fields made significant connections and influenced each other. This study makes a valuable contribution to the understanding of the relevance of the arts to humanistic psychology, and demonstrates the importance of a psychology that acknowledges cultural trends as diagnostic and prognostic of individual psychological issues.

I hope that this research study will serve as a catalyst, and encourage other researchers to explore this area of inquiry, initiating further examinations of these connections and trends. There are many themes that could be developed. For example, I might return to the research participants to investigate the ways in which their various mentors shaped their professional work. The psychotherapeutic connections should again be explored.

Another research study could examine other areas of the art world. For example, might painters and sculptors be more cognizant of humanistic psychology than the dancers were? And what role might the art therapists play in establishing these connections?

A third study might explore such questions as: are members of the creative arts communities (individually and collectively) more aware of and more involved in humanistic psychology than those working in other fields, such as physics or chemistry (the hard sciences), the business community, or the field of education?

My hope is that this research study will initiate further exploration and examination of the connections between the creative arts and humanistic psychology.

References

ADTA. (2001). *Fact Sheet.* Columbia, MD: The American Dance Therapy Association.

Anderson, J. (1997). *Art without boundaries: The world of modern dance.* Iowa City: University of Iowa Press.

Benbow-Niemier, G. (1998). Wigman, Mary: German modern dance pioneer, choreographer, and educator. In T. Benbow-Pfalzgraf (Ed.), *International dictionary of modern dance* (pp.822-824). Detroit, MI: St. James Press.

Bernstein, P. L. (Ed.). (1979). *Eight theoretical approaches in dance-movement therapy.* Dubuque, IA: Kendall-Hunt.

Boyatzis, R. E. (1998). *Transforming qualitative information: Thematic analysis and code development.* Thousand Oaks, CA: Sage.

Bremser, M. (1999). (Ed.) *Fifty contemporary choreographers.* London: Routledge.

Brown, J. M., Mindlin, N., & Woodford, C. H., (Eds.). (1979). 2nd Ed. *The vision of modern dance: in the words of its creators.* Hightstown NJ: Princeton, Book Co.

Bruch, H. (1973). *Eating disorders.* New York: Basic Books.

Bugental, J. F. T. (1981). *The search for authenticity: An existential-analytic approach to psychotherapy.* New York: Irvington Publishers, Inc. (Original work published 1965)

Bugental, J. F. T. (1987). *The art of the psychotherapist.* New York: Norton.

Bugental, J. F. T. (1999). *Psychotherapy isn't what you think.* Phoenix, AZ: Zeig, Tucker & Co.

Campbell, J. (1949). *The hero of a thousand faces.* New York: Pantheon.

Campbell, M. (1999). Martha Graham: An American Original. *Dance Magazine, 73*(3), pp.72-75.

Capacchione, L. (1979). *The creative journal: The art of finding yourself.* Athens: Ohio University Press

Chace, M. (1964). Dance alone is not enough. *Dance Magazine, 38*(4), 46, 47, 58.

Chace, M. (1975). Dance as an adjunctive therapy with hospitalized mental patients. In H. Chaiklin (Ed.), *Marian Chace: Her papers* (pp.70-77). Columbia, MD: The American Dance Therapy Association. (Original work published 1953)

Chace, M. (1975). Untitled article on professional history. In H. Chaiklin (Ed.), *Marian Chace: Her papers* (pp.15-19). Columbia, MD: The American Dance Therapy Association.

Chace, M. (1993). Untitled articles on professional history. In S. L. Sandel, S. Chaiklin, & A. Lohn (Eds.), *Foundations of dance/movement therapy: The life and work of Marian Chace* (pp.12-19). Columbia, MD: The Marian Chace Memorial Fund of the American Dance Therapy Association.

Chapman, A. H. (1976). *Harry Stack Sullivan: His life and his work.* New York: G. P. Putnam & Sons.

Cristofori, M. (1998). Holm, Hanya: German choreographer, dancer, educator, stage director and company director. In T. Benbow-Pfalzgraf (Ed.), *International dictionary of modern dance* (pp.355-359). Detroit, MI: St. James Press.

deCarvalho, R. J. (1991). *The founders of humanistic psychology.* New York: Praeger.

DeFrantz, T. (1998), Pilobolus Dance Theater, American dance company. In T. Benbow-Pfalzgraf (Ed.), *International dictionary of modern dance* (pp.631-634). Detroit, MI: St. James Press.

Dell, C. (1970). *A primer for movement description.* New York: Dance Notation Bureau.

deMille, A. (1991). *Martha, the life and work of Martha Graham.* New York: Random House.

Evans, R. I. (1975). *Carl Rogers: The man and his ideas.* New York: E. P. Dutton & Co., Inc.

Ferenczi, S. (1955). The principles and relaxation and neo-catharsis. In M. Balint (Ed.), *Final contributions to the problems and methods of psychoanalysis* (pp. 108-125). London: The Hogarth Press & The Institute of Psychoanalysis. (Original work published 1929)

Ferenczi, S. & Rank, O. (1925). *The development of psychoanalysis.* New York: Nervous and Mental Diseases Publishing.

Fraleigh, S. H. (1987). *Dance and the lived body.* Pittsburgh, PA: University of Pittsburgh Press.

Frank, J. D., & Frank, J. B. (1991). *Persuasion and healing: A comparative study of psychotherapy.* Baltimore, MD: Johns Hopkins University Press.

Flitch, J. E. C. (1912). *Modern dancing and dancers.* Philadelphia: J. B. Lippincott Co.

Fromm-Reichmann, F. (1950). *Principles of intensive psychotherapy.* Chicago: University of Chicago Press.

Garafola, L. (2001). Excellence light and dark. *Dance, 75*(3), 84-85.

Gilbert, F. (1976). *Jazz, rock and roll, and the revolution in psychotherapy.* Unpublished doctoral dissertation, Humanistic Psychology Institute, San Francisco, CA.

Goldberg, M. (1999). Trisha Brown. In M. Bremser, (Ed.), *Fifty contemporary choreographers* (pp. 37-42). London: Routledge.

Gould, N. & Shawn, T. (1912). Interpretive and Classic DANCERS and Teachers of Interpretive and Classic Dancing. Studio, 1615 Georgia Street, Los Angeles, California, Phone, 2249. Printed advertisement found in the personal files of Ted Shawn. Archived at Jacob's Pillow.

Graham, M. (1998). Graham 1937. In J. M.Brown, N. Mindlin, & C. H. Woodford, (Eds.), *The vision of modern dance in the words of its creators* (2nd ed., pp.49-53). Hightstown, NJ: Princeton Book Co. (Original work published 1979)

Graham, M. (1973). *The notebooks of Martha Graham.* New York: Harcourt, Brace, Janovich, Inc.

Greening, T. (2001). Five basic postulates of humanistic psychology. *Journal of Humanistic Psychology, 41*(3), 3.

Grosskurth, P. (1991). *The secret ring: Freud's inner circle and the politics of psychoanalysis.* Reading, PA: Addison-Wesley.

Guest, A. H. (1989). *Limón-based modern dance technique.* Surrey, England: Cevera Press.

Hale, N. G., Jr. (1995). *The rise and crisis of psychoanalysis in the United States: Freud and the Americans, 1917-1985.* New York: Oxford University Press.

Harris, J. (1999). Murray Louis. In M. Bremser (Ed.), *Fifty contemporary choreographers* (pp.141-145). London: Routledge

Herrigel, E. (1971). *Zen in the art of archery.* New York: Random House. (Original work published 1953)

Hoffman, E. (1988). *The right to be human.* Los Angeles: Jeremy P. Tarcher.

Hoffman, H. (1996a). *Humanistic psychology, assignment #1.* Unpublished manuscript. Saybrook Graduate School and Research Center, San Francisco.

Hoffman, H. (1996b). *Humanistic psychology, assignment #2.* Unpublished manuscript. Saybrook Graduate School and Research Center, San Francisco.

Hoffman, H. (1997). *Advanced humanistic psychology.* Unpublished manuscript. Saybrook Graduate School and Research Center, San Francisco.

Hoffman, H. (1999a). *Research practicum.* Unpublished manuscript. Saybrook Graduate School and Research Center, San Francisco, CA.

Hoffman, H. (1999b). *Sandor Ferenczi and the humanistic psychologists.* Unpublished manuscript. Saybrook Graduate School and Research Center, San Francisco, CA.

Hoffman, H. (1999c). *Marian Chace: The bridge between dance and psychology.* Unpublished manuscript. Saybrook Graduate School and Research Center, San Francisco, CA.

Hoffman, H. (2003). Sandor Ferenczi and the Origins of Humanistic Psychology, *Journal of Humanistic Psychology.* 4, 59-86.

Holm, H. (1935). The German Dance in the American Scene. In V. Stewart (Ed.), *Modern dance* (pp. 79-86). New York: E. Weyle.

Holm, H. (1951). The Mary Wigman I know. In W. Sorell (Ed.), *The dance has many faces* (3rd rev., pp.18-27). Chicago: A capella Books.

Horst, L., & Russell, C. (1967). *Modern dance forms in relation to the other modern arts.* Brooklyn, NY: Dance Horizons. (Original work published 1961)

Hutchinson, A. (1970). Labanotation; or Kinetography Laban: The system for recording movement. (Rev. and exp.). New York: Theatre Arts Books.

Hutchinson, A., (1970). *Labanotation, Kinetography Laban: The System for recording movement.*

Jacob's Ladder Trail Mobile Exhibition, June 15-September 1, 2001. On display at Blake's Barn, Jacob's Pillow, Lee, MA.

Jowitt, D. (1985). Portrait of the artist as survivor. In D. Jowitt (Ed.), *The dance in mind: Profiles and reviews 1976-83* (pp. 287-292). Boston: D. R. Godine.

Kendall, E. (1979). *Where she danced.* New York: Alfred A. Knopf.

Kisselgoff, A. (2000, December 11). Distilling the passionate essence of broken love. *The New York Times,* p. E10.

Kirschenbaum, H., & Henderson, V. L. (Eds.). (1989). *The Carl Rogers reader.* New York: Houghton Mifflin.

Knight, J. (1998). Nagrin, Daniel: American dancer, choreographer, educator, and writer. In T. Benbow-Pfalzgraph (Ed.), *International dictionary of modern dance* (pp. 570-572). Detroit, MI: St. James Press.

Laban, R. (1971). *The Mastery of movement* (3rd ed.). Boston: Plays, Inc. (Original work published 1950)

Legge, T. (1963). *The I Ching: The book of changes.* (J. Legge, Trans.). New York: Dover. (Original work published 1899)

Levy, F. (1988). *Dance/movement therapy: A healing art.* Reston, VA: The American Alliance for Health, Physical Education, Recreation, and Dance.

Lewis, P. (1993). The use of Chace techniques in the depth dance therapy process of recovery, healing and spiritual consciousness. In S. L. Sandel, S. Chaiklin, & A. Lohn (Eds.), *Foundations of dance/movement therapy: The life and work of Marian Chace* (pp.154-167). Columbia, MD: The Marian Chace Memorial Fund of the American Dance Therapy Association

Long, B. (1998). Tetley, Glen, American dancer, choreographer, and company director. In T. Benbow-Pfalzgraf (Ed.), *International dictionary of modern dance* (pp. 765-769). Detroit, MI: St. James Press.

Luborsky, M. (1994). The identification of themes and patterns. In J. Gubrium & A. Sankar (Eds.), *Qualitative methods in aging research* (pp.189-210). Thousand Oaks, CA: Sage.

Luzzatto. P. (1995). The mental double trap of the anorexic patient. In D. Doktor (Ed.), *Arts therapies and clients with eating disorders. Fragile board* (pp.60-75). London: Jessica Kingsley.

Marcotty, F. (1998). Schonberg, Bessie, German-born American dancer and Educator. In T. Benbow-Pfalzgraf (Ed.), *International dictionary of modern dance* (pp.701-702). Detroit, MI: St. James Press.

Maslow, A. H. (1957). A philosophy of psychology: The need of a mature science of human nature. In F. T. Severin (Ed.), *Humanistic viewpoints in psychology* (pp.17-32). New York: McGraw-Hill.

Maslow, A. H. (1961). Health as transcendence of environment. *Journal of Humanistic Psychology, 1*(1), 1-7.

Maslow, A. H. (1971). *The farther reaches of human nature.* New York: Van Nostrand Reinhold.

Maslow, A. H. (1986). *Toward a psychology of being* (2nd ed.). New York: Van Nostrand Reinhold.

May, R. (1939). *The Art of counseling.* Nashville, TENN: Abingdon Press.

May, R. (1966). The problem of will and intentionality in psychoanalysis. *Contemporary Psychoanalysis, 3*(2), 55-70.

May, R. (1969). *Love and will.* New York: W. W. Norton.

May, R. (1970). Psychology and the daimonic. In J. Campbell (Ed.), *Myths, dreams and religion* (pp.196-210). New York: E. P. Dutton.

May, R. (1975). *The courage to create.* New York: W.W. Norton.

May, R. (1985). *My quest for beauty.* San Francisco: Saybrook.

May, R. (1991). *The cry for myth.* New York: W. W. Norton.

Maynard, O. (1965). *American modern dancers: The pioneers.* Boston: Little, Brown.

McDonagh, D. (1970). *The rise and fall of modern dance.* New York: E. P. Dutton.

McDonagh, D. (1973). *Martha Graham.* New York: Praeger.

McDonagh, D. (1976). *The complete guide to modern dance.* Garden City, NY: Doubleday.

Miles, M.B., & Huberman, A.M. (1994). *Qualitative data analysis: An expanded sourcebook,* (2nd ed.). Thousand Oaks, CA: Sage.

Minderovic, C. M. (1998). Louis, Murray. In T. Benbow-Pfalzgraf (Ed.), *International dictionary of modern dance* (pp.496-499). Detroit, MI: St. James Press.

Minuchin, S., & Nichols, M. P. (1993). *Family healing: Tales of hope and renewal from family therapy.* New York: The Free Press.

Montuori, A., & Purser, R. E. (1995). Deconstructing the lone genius myth: Toward a contextual view of creativity. *Journal of Humanistic Psychology, 35*(3), 69-112.

Mooney, R. L. (1963). A conceptual model for integrating four approaches to the identification of creative talent. In C. W. Taylor & F. Barron (Eds.), *Scientific creativity: Its recognition and development* (pp.331-340). New York: Wiley.

Owen, N. (1997a). *A certain place: The Jacob's Pillow story.* Becket, MA: Jacob's Pillow Dance Festival.

Owen, N. (1997b). Crossroads of the dance world. *Dance, 71*(6), 62-69.

Owen, N. (2002). *A certain place: The Jacob's Pillow Story* (rev. ed.). Becket, MA: Jacob's Pillow.

Pace, E. (1994, October 24). Dr. Rollo May is dead at 85; Was innovator in psychology. *The New York Times,* p. B12.

Pierpont, M. (1980). A conversation with Irmgard Bartenenieff. *Dance, 54*(3), 90-91.

Poindexter, B. (1963). *Ted Shawn: His personal life, his professional career, and his contributions to the development of dance in the United States of America from 1891-1963.* Unpublished doctoral dissertation, Texas Women's University, College of Health, Physical Education and Recreation. Denton, TX.

Raugust, K. (1998). Lamhut, Phyllis, American dancer and choreographer. In T. Benbow-Pfalzgraf (Ed.), *International dictionary of American dance* (pp.451-454). Detroit, MI: St. James Press.

Raugust, K., & Benet, S. (1998). Redlich, Don: American dancer, choreographer, and company director. In T. Benbow-Pfalzgraf (Ed.), *International dictionary of modern dance* (pp. 664-667). Detroit, MI: St. James Press.

Reich, S. (1973). Notes on music and dance. In R. Copeland & M. Cohen (Eds.), *What is dance? Readings in theory and criticism* (1983; pp.336-338). New York: Oxford University Press.

Reich, W. (1990). *Character analysis.* New York: Noonday Press, Farrar, Straus & Giroux. (Original work published 1945)

Rogers, C. R. (1942). *Counseling and psychotherapy: Newer concepts in practice.* Boston: Houghton Mifflin

Rogers, C. R. (1951). *Client-centered therapy: Its current practice, implications, and theory.* Boston: Houghton-Mifflin.

Rogers, C. R. (1957). *The Humanist, 17,* 291-300.

Rogers, C. R. (1958). A process conception of psychotherapy. *American Psychologist. 13,* 142-149.

Rogers, C. R. (1961). *On becoming a person: A therapist's view of psychotherapy.* Boston: Houghton Mifflin.

Rogers, C. R. (1963). Learning to be free. In S. M. Farber & R. H. Wilson (Eds.), *Conflict and creativity: Control of the mind* (pt. 2, pp.268-288). New York: McGraw-Hill.

Rogers, C. R. (1970). *Carl Rogers on encounter groups.* New York: Harper & Row.

Rogers, C. R. (1975). Empathic: An unappreciated way of being. *The Counseling Psychologist,* 5(2), pp. 2-10.

Rogers, C. R. (1977). *Carl Rogers on personal power.* New York: Delacorte Press.

Rogers, C. R. (1986). A client-centered person-centered approach to therapy. In I. Kutash & A. Wolfe (Eds.), *Psychotherapists' casebook* (pp.197-208). San Francisco: Jossey-Bass.

Rubin, H. J., & Rubin, I. S. (1995). *Qualitative interviewing: The art of hearing data.* Thousand Oaks, CA: Sage.

Ruggiero, A. (1998). DeLavallade, Carmen, American dancer, choreographer, and educator. In T. Benbow-Pfalzgraf (Ed.), *International dictionary of modern dance* (pp.180-190). Detroit, MI: St. James Press.

Runco, M. A., & Richards, R. (1997). *Eminent creativity, everyday creativity, and health.* Greenwich, CT: Ablex Publishing.

Schlundt, C. L. (1962). *A chronology of the professional appearances of the American dancers Ruth St. Denis & Ted Shawn, 1906-1932.* New York: New York Public Library.

Scanlon, J. (1995). Biography prepared by Norton Owen for the José Limón Foundation, New York City.

Schneider, K. J., Bugental, J. F. T., & Pierson, J. F., (Eds.). (2001). *The handbook of humanistic psychology: Leading edges in theory, research and practice.* Thousand Oaks, CA: Sage.

Schneider, K. J., & May, R. (1995). *The psychology of existence: An integrative, clinical perspective.* New York: McGraw-Hill.

Schwartz, G. E., & Kine, J. P. (1997). Repression, emotional disclosure, and health: Theoretical, empirical, and clinical considerations. In J. W. Pennebaker (Ed.), *Emotional disclosures and health* (pp.177-193). Washington, DC: American Psychological Association.

Serlin, I. (1989). Movement composition and the choreography of a verbal psychotherapy session. In A. Robbins (Ed.), *The psychoaesthetic experience: An approach to depth-oriented treatment* (pp.45-57). New York: Human Sciences Press.

Serlin, I. (1990). Therapy with a borderline nun. *Psychotherapy, 27*(1), 91-94.

Shawn, T. (1940). *Dance we must: Lectures delivered at George Peabody College in Nashville, Tenn., June 13-July 2, 1938.* Pittsfield, MA: Eagle Printing & Binding.

Shawn, T. (1947). *How beautiful upon the mountain* (3rd ed.). Monograph, privately printed, archived at Jacob's Pillow.

Shawn, T. (1957, January 9). Letter from Ted Shawn to LeRoy Leatherman, archived at Jacob's Pillow.

Shawn, T. (1960a). *One thousand and one night stands.* Garden City, NY: Doubleday.
Shawn, T. (1960b). Flyer advertising Martha Graham's appearance at Jacob's Pillow. Archived at Jacob's Pillow.

Shawn, T. (1963). *Every little movement.* Pittsfield, MA: Eagle Printing & Binding. (Original work published 1954)

Shelton, S. (1981). *Divine dancer: A biography of Ruth St. Denis.* New York: Doubleday.

Sherman, J., & Mumaw, B. (2000). *Barton Mumaw, Dancer.* Hanover, NH: Wesleyan University Press.

Siegel, M. B. (1979). *The shapes of change: Images of American dance.* Boston: Houghton-Mifflin.

Sorell, W. (1969). *Hanya Holm: The biography of an artist.* Middletown, CT: Wesleyan University Press.

Sorell, W. (1973). *The Mary Wigman Book: Her writings edited and translated.* Middletown, CT: Wesleyan University Press.

Stark, A., Aronow, S., & T. McGeehan. (1989). Dance/movement therapy with bulemic patients. In L.M. Hornyak & E.K. Baker (Eds.), *Experiential therapies for eating disorders* (pp.121-143). New York: Guilford Press.

Stebbins, G. (1902). *Delsarte systems of expression* (rev .ed.). New York: Edgar S. Werner.
St. Denis, R. (1932). *Lotus light.* Cambridge: The Riverside Press.

St. Denis, R. (1939). *An unfinished life.* New York: Harper and Brothers.

St. Denis, R. (1997). In K. Miller (Ed.), *Wisdom comes dancing: Selected writings of Ruth St. Denis on dance, spirituality and the body.* Seattle, WA: PeaceWorks

Stodelle, E. (1984*). Deep song: The dance story of Martha Graham.* New York: Schirmer Books.

Stone, H., & S. Stone, (1989). *Embracing our selves: The voice dialogue manual.* Novato, CA: New World Library. (Original work published 1985)

Solomons, Jr., G. (2001, February 11). Against the odds, they keep on making dance. *The New York Times,* pp. AR 34-35.

Taper, B. (1996). *Balanchine, a biography* (2nd ed.). Los Angeles: University of California Press.

Terry, W. (1941, July 12). The dance. *The New York Herald Tribune* (n.p., archived at Jacob's Pillow).

Terry, W. (1956). *The dance in America.* New York: Harper & Row.

Terry, W. (1976). *Ted Shawn, father of American dance.* New York: Dial Press.

Timm, F. (1996). A celebration of life and dance. *Dance, 70*(12), 60-64.

Tracy, R. (1999). Celebrating Carmen deLavallade's fifty-year career. *Dance, 73*(8), 37.

Von Laban, R. (1971). The Mastery of movement.

Wigman, M. (1986). *Mary Wigman: The language of dance.* Middletown, CT: Wesleyan University Press. (Original work published 1963)

INDEX

STUDIES IN DANCE